M000266033

BLACK WOMEN WRITERS
OF LOUISIANA

BLACK WOMEN WRITERS
OF LOUISIANA

TELLING THEIR STORIES

ANN B. DOBIE

ILLUSTRATIONS BY DAREN TUCKER | FOREWORD BY PHEBE A. HAYES, PHD,
FOUNDER AND PRESIDENT, IBERIA AFRICAN AMERICAN HISTORICAL SOCIETY

THE
History
PRESS

Published by The History Press
Charleston, SC
www.historypress.com

Copyright © 2022 by Ann B. Dobie
All rights reserved

All artwork by Daren Tucker.

First published 2022

Manufactured in the United States

ISBN 9781467151719

Library of Congress Control Number: 2021949171

CONTENTS

FOREWORD

I am honored to have been asked to write the foreword for *Black Women Writers of Louisiana: Telling Their Stories*. In this new text, Ann Dobie curates an impressive collection of African American women writers of Louisiana, many of whom may have been otherwise forgotten. Unfortunately, early historians have ignored or marginalized the experiences and contributions of Louisiana's African American citizens. Research that uncovers these contributions is sorely needed so that we may honor that history and collectively work toward racial reconciliation.

Since retiring from academia in 2013, I have also devoted myself to uncovering the hidden histories of African Americans in Louisiana. In 2018, I founded a nonprofit organization, the Iberia African American Historical Society (IAAHS), the mission of which is to research, teach and commemorate the true and inclusive history of Iberia Parish. In our early research, the society discovered that the first African American woman to earn a medical degree in Louisiana and practice medicine was Dr. Emma Wakefield Paillet, born in New Iberia, Louisiana, in 1868. This uncovered history is reminiscent of one of the women featured in this text, Alice Ruth Moore Dunbar-Nelson, who was born in 1875. Given that they were contemporaries, it is possible that they knew each other. Both attended Straight University in New Orleans, both were born in Acadiana, both were mixed-race and both were classically trained musicians. Both deserve to have their stories told.

Ann Dobie's efforts to educate the public about the long and rich histories of African American women writers in Louisiana is important, necessary and enlightening. This is a collection that is long overdue. Besides the general public, I believe educators will appreciate the work she has done to make this collection available. It is her effort to bring these women's untold history to the public's attention that hooked me from the first few seconds I learned of it, and I have no doubt that as the reader, you will be hooked, too.

—Phebe A. Hayes, PhD
Founder and President
The Iberia African American Historical Society

PREFACE

Louisiana has a rich literary history, but it is not necessarily a well-known one. On occasion, I have referred to it as one of the state's most overlooked natural resources. Most of the attention it has garnered has been directed primarily to the works of white male writers, the stories, poems and plays of more marginalized groups having received less notice. One group that has been relatively overlooked is Louisiana's Black women writers, who belong to two sub-groups, those defined by gender and by race.

In their study *Louisiana Women Writers*, Dorothy H. Brown and Barbara C. Ewell note the lack critical attention given to non-white Louisiana writers. They specifically lament "the paucity of scholarship on Louisiana's African-American women, especially since in the last twenty years that group has produced such a flowering of poets and playwrights." Brown and Ewell are correct on two points: the state's Black women writers have escaped notice, and their history is not a long one. Due to lack of education and opportunity, their record is fairly brief. The earliest writer of note was Alice Ruth Dunbar Nelson, a fiery activist, columnist and storyteller whose work began in the late nineteenth century. With time, that situation has changed dramatically, as the list of colleges and universities attended by those represented here shows, with the result that today's Black women writers are not only receiving prestigious awards and honors but also finding a general readership that puts them at the forefront of the national literary scene.

This new crop of writers is marked by their passion and their imagination. On occasion, their urgency is gritty, even brutal, but it is born of the need to tell overlooked stories and call attention to social wrongs. Sarah Broom's remembrance of her childhood home in New Orleans East is sometimes painful but always honest. Even the gentler narratives, such as Ladee Hubbard's *Introducing the Ribkins* or the quiet poems of Pinkie

Gordon Lane that speak of lives lived in family love and support, are filled with emotional power and warmth. And even they acknowledge the difficult circumstances that surround the lives they depict. The stories they tell are marked by authenticity, even those that invoke the surreal. In *Sing, Unburied, Sing*, for example, Jesmyn Ward's introduction of the ghost of Richie, a young boy who served time in Parchman Prison, is believable because the tales he tells are true.

Although today's writers hold such characteristics in common, they are also marked by significant diversity. They come from cities and small towns, champion different causes and work in a variety of genres. Many of them are from New Orleans or its surrounding area. Almost all of them are from South Louisiana, but within that region, they hail from small towns, like Elizabeth Brown-Guillory's hometown of Church Point, as well as cities, their works reflecting life as it is lived in rural as well as urban areas. Their causes range from the efforts of Sybil Kein to promote Creole culture—its history, language and customs—to Mona Lisa Saloy's poems that record everyday life. And their various points of view are set down in poems, plays, stories and essays. Within their commonality, they represent a broad spectrum of experience and belief.

It is hoped that in years to come, additional studies like *Black Women Writers of Louisiana* will ensue. The talent represented by the twelve playwrights, poets and storytellers featured here will no doubt be followed by that of other Black women writers who will give readers additional insights into the Black experience—into the human experience. I expect this look at their work to be one of a long line of such studies as readers and critics alike will surely acknowledge the quality of their efforts.

ACKNOWLEDGEMENTS

Books carry an author's name on their front covers, their back covers and their title pages. The practice seems to announce that what is published is the product of a single mind, the efforts of one person. Such is not the case. Books are influenced by other people and events that play an invaluable role in creating them. In the case of *Black Women Writers of Louisiana: Telling Their Stories*, help has come from numerous sources, and I am grateful for them all.

Adding perspective to my text is the foreword by Phebe Hayes. Her experience of founding and working with the Iberia African American Historical Society to unearth stories of past generations of people of color living in her deeply southern parish has resulted in social acknowledgment of the significance of their contributions to its history. Her knowledge and expertise have also contributed to my understanding of stories told by the authors studied here. I thank her.

Daren Tucker has contributed to the written words that compose this book by using her artistic talent to render images of the profiled writers. When I ran into difficulty in using photographs of them, she came to my aid by creating the pen-and-ink drawings that introduce each one. To me, the ability to reproduce an image is akin to magic. I can neither understand how it happens nor do it myself. I marvel at her work and am grateful for it.

The friends and family who have listened to my reports on the journey of discovery that has characterized the writing of this book are to be doubly thanked. They have listened patiently and intently, sometimes making suggestions as to elements that worked and, most helpfully, elements that did not accomplish what was intended. Two who come to mind are my dear friends the Reverend Honey Becker and retired judge Anne Simon. Their comments and suggestions have pushed me along time and again.

Looking to the future, I will be grateful to those who find this book useful. I hope it spreads the news that Louisiana is home to a host of highly talented Black women writers who through their poems, plays, fiction and nonfiction help us to understand the culture in which we live.

ALICE RUTH MOORE DUNBAR-NELSON

A WOMAN BEFORE HER TIME

Alice Ruth Moore Dunbar-Nelson challenged, and broke, every stereotype placed on Black women, fighting constantly for her independence against the trammels of racism.
—Adrienne Rich

Alice Ruth Moore Dunbar-Nelson was a woman with several names and even more professions. She was a poet, teacher, journalist, platform speaker, political activist, stenographer, executive secretary, editor, newspaper columnist and campaign manager, none of which was a likely career for a mixed-race woman born in 1875, even one living in multicultural New Orleans. The daughter of a seamstress who was a former slave born in Opelousas, Louisiana, and a father who was a white seaman of New Orleans, she recalled in adulthood being rejected by both races as too white to do the work of Blacks and too Black to be worthy of white work.

Despite such seeming drawbacks, in 1892, Dunbar completed a two-year teacher-training program at Straight University (which later merged into Dillard University) and began teaching in the public school system of New Orleans at Old Marigny Elementary. In this position, she assumed a prominent place in Creole society, especially in musical and literary circles. Teaching made her a living, but it is for her writing that she is remembered today. She wrote in many genres wherever she was and whatever else she was doing.

From her girlhood in New Orleans on, she participated in amateur theater. Later, she wrote and directed plays and pageants for school and community groups. In the African American community, she wrote skits and plays for class night programs, for Christmas and Easter celebrations and for club fundraising attractions. Whereas characters in her fiction are not identified as Black, those in her plays are, and through them she worked to broaden their stereotypical presentations. In adulthood, most of her plays were never presented, the best known one being *Mine Eyes Have Seen*. She even tried out silent films, without success.

In a few years, she left New Orleans for Boston and then moved on to New York. When her writing and a photograph in a literary magazine caught the attention of Paul Laurence Dunbar, he began a correspondence with her that went on for two years. In 1898, she moved to Washington, D.C., to be with him, and they married that year. As Paul Dunbar was America's first celebrated Black poet, he was prominent in the Harlem Renaissance, drawing her into the intellectual, social and artistic movement known at the time as the New Negro Movement. She also taught in Brooklyn, as she would continue doing in different schools at the elementary, secondary and college levels until 1931.

The marriage was unsuccessful, even tempestuous, due partly to Paul's tuberculosis, depression and alcoholism. (Doctors prescribed alcohol to treat his tuberculosis, and he became addicted.) He was also disturbed by her lesbian affairs and was frequently absent from the marriage due to his career. She left him after he beat her severely in 1902 and moved to Delaware. They were never divorced but remained separated. He died in 1906.

In Delaware, she taught at Howard High School in Wilmington for over a decade. She not only taught but also became head of the English Department, raised money, directed class night plays, wrote the history of the school and assisted the administration. Later, she would write an (unpublished) novel titled *This Lofty Oak* about the founder of Howard High School, who gave Dunbar emotional support and encouragement. She also taught summer sessions at State College for Colored Students (now Delaware State University) and at the Hampton Institute. She enrolled as a student at Cornell University in 1907 and then went back to Delaware. On her return, she married Henry Arthur Callis, a prominent physician and professor at Howard University, but kept it secret. It quickly ended in divorce, perhaps because he was twelve years younger than she but also because she continued to pursue physical and emotional relationships with other women. (In her diary, she alludes to such affairs and flirtations.)

In 1916, Alice Dunbar-Nelson was married a third time to Robert J. Nelson, whom she called Bobbo, a journalist, poet, civil rights activist and widower with two children. Their marriage has been described by Gloria Hull as "a good professional union." They stayed married, although she had intimate relations with several women during this time. She joined Nelson in his activism and was involved in many civic, racial and women's causes.

Despite her hyperactive lifestyle, she had a variety of health problems: high blood pressure, apoplectic spells, kidney albumen, neuritis and sciatica, vertigo, fatigue, leucorrhea and insomnia. In 1930, she complained in her diary of mental distress: "profoundly in the D's—discouraged, depressed, disheartened, disgusted." Throughout the diary, she complains of having "the blues" and worries about growing old, being "unestablished," middle-aged and able to remain useful.

Her busy life ended in 1935 due to a heart ailment at the age of sixty. Her papers were collected by the University of Delaware. Throughout her life, she received more public notice for being Paul Dunbar's wife than for her own achievement, but today, she is remembered for her writing and her fight for social justice for women and African Americans.

Alice Dunbar was obviously intelligent, but she had additional attributes that helped her make her way in the world. She was described by family and friends as being forceful and strong willed, imaginative and inquisitive. It did not hurt that she was also tall, light skinned enough to pass for white, had auburn curls and dressed in an elegant fashion. At times, she seemed to be highly emotional, needing a calming influence around her. In fact, her personality was full of contrasts, even contradictions. For example, she was said to be very ladylike, conscious of her reputation, her good manners and social conventions. She had the education, culture, looks and manner of "the higher classes," but according to Hull, she also liked to drink bootleg whiskey, go to Harlem clubs and cabarets, play the numbers and wear "hot clothes." Indeed, she thought of herself as belonging to the upper class although she was not financially secure, having sometimes to go to pawnshops to get money to pay her household bills. She had a lifelong interest in psychology and used unorthodox spiritual systems. She believed in "bad-mouthing" (speaking curses on deserving people), read her future in cards, paid attention to her dreams and relied heavily on her unconscious mind.

Although Dunbar played many roles throughout her lifetime, it is for her writings that she is chiefly remembered today. Journalism, which took most of her time, fit her talents and needs. In her newspaper columns, she spoke from a Black woman's point of view, allowing herself to be contrary, witty, iconoclastic and intellectual. It allowed her space to indulge the causes that occupied her for so many years, particularly race and feminism. At the same time, she also worked at short stories, poetry, film scenarios, plays, fiction and a diary and started at least four novels. In addition, she edited two anthologies. Unfortunately, journalism was not as highly regarded by readers and critics as fiction and poetry, but she regarded all her work as "producing literature."

Dunbar's first collection of stories and poems, *Violets and Other Tales*, was published in 1898 by *The Monthly Review* when she was barely twenty years old. It is an early example of her ability to work in multiple genres, as it is a collection of short stories, sketches, essays, reviews and poetry, some of the pieces probably written for newspapers or magazines. In subjects and style, they are similar to other works of their day except for their depiction of Creole culture. Several of the stories are set in New Orleans with the characters living in its neighborhoods, walking its streets and passing its landmarks. Typical is "Anarchy Alley," which describes a small part of the city as a sort of Bohemia in America:

> *Plenty of saloons—great, gorgeous, gaudy places, with pianos and swift-footed waiters, tables and cards, and men, men, men. The famous Three Brothers Saloon occupies a position about midway the alley, and at its doors, the acme, the culminating point, the superlative degree of unquietude and discontent is reached....Behind its odors, swinging as easily between the street and the liquor-fumed halls as the soul swings between right and wrong, the disturbed minds of the working-men become clouded, heated, and wrothily ready for deeds of violence.*

Four years after publication of *Violets*, she brought out what was to become one of her most admired works, *The Goodness of St. Roque, and Other Stories*, although it was barely noticed at the time. She published it as a companion piece to her husband's (Paul Laurence Dunbar) *Poems of Cabin and Field*. In this volume, she continued to mine her Creole heritage, making her one of the first Louisiana women of color to publish books in English and to explore Creole society. The title story, for example, traces the route of the train that

> *puffed its way wheezily out wide Elysian Fields Street, around the lily-covered bayous, to Milneburg-on-the-Lake. Now a picnic at Milneburg is a thing to be remembered for ever. One charters a rickety-looking, weather-beaten dancing pavilion, built over the water, and after storing the*

children—for your true Creole never leaves the small folks at home—and the baskets and mothers downstairs, the young folks go upstairs and dance to the tune of the best band you ever heard. For what can equal the music of a violin, a guitar, a cornet, and a bass viol to trip the quadrille to at a picnic?

"A Carnival Jangle" is a sketch of a Mardi Gras in New Orleans where the fun ends in a mistaken murder of a young girl. Dunbar portrays the city during the season as follows:

A madding dream of color and melody and fantasy gone wild. The streets a crush of jesters and maskers, Jim Crows and clowns, ballet girls and Mephistos, Indians and monkeys; of wild and sudden flashes of music, of glittering pageants and comic ones, of befeathered and belled horses, an effervescent bubble of beauty that shifts and changes and passes kaleidoscope-like before the bewildered eye.

In short, Dunbar, undoubtedly influenced by the success of Grace King and Kate Chopin, capitalized on the attraction readers, and therefore publishers, had to the seemingly exotic people and practices of New Orleans in general and Creole culture in particular. As one contemporary reviewer wrote in the Pittsburgh *Christian Advocate* in December 1899: "delightful Creole stories, all bright and full of the true Creole air of easy-going…brief and pleasing, instinct with the passion and romance of people who will ever be associated with such names as Bayou Teche and Lake Pontchartrain." Nevertheless, beneath the surface charm of her stories, one senses darkness. In "On the Bayou Bridge," for example, she describes Bayou St. John as darkly mysterious. "In its dark bosom many secrets lie buried. It is like some beautiful serpent, languorous, sinister. It ripples in the sunshine, sparkles in the moonlight, glooms in the dusk and broods in the dark. But it thinks unceasingly, and below its brightest sparkle you feel its unknown soul."

In her stories, Dunbar hints at some of the issues she faces more directly in her essays and newspaper columns, although what was only suggested in her early fiction does become more overt later on. She paid little attention, for example, to racial issues in her fiction and even obscured her own status as a woman of color by identifying with her white Creole characters. Any reference to racial oppression or injustice is indirect and subtle. She concentrates on a mixed-race society, Creole society, which for her always included people of color. In stories such as "Elisabeth" and "Ellen Fenton," she hints at feminist issues, such as discontent with the limited role of the married woman, and racism is present in "Nathalie." In general, however, Dunbar's stories refrain from direct argument, perhaps due in part to publishers' unwillingness to publish stories about controversial topics.

Dunbar flourished during the Harlem Renaissance, in part due to her husband's reputation in the movement. Although she was not considered a major figure for her own literary contributions, she influenced the work of other Black writers by her publications and by her reviews of such writers as Langston Hughes. Through her involvement with the Harlem Renaissance, she was able to publish more of her poetry, which is marked by conventional lyric themes and styles typical of female writers at that time, characteristics that today often seem overwrought, too emotional and sentimental.

Dunbar was more willing to take on controversial topics in her articles and public speeches. In particular, she was not timid about discussing her support of feminism and racial justice. Her involvement with such causes started to appear around 1900, when she began to speak about women's suffrage. It then appeared in articles that she wrote or co-edited such as "Negro Women in War Work" (1919) and "Politics in Delaware" (1924). In "Is It Time for Negro Colleges in the South to Be Put in the Hands of Negro Teachers?" she explored the role of Black women in the workforce, education and the anti-lynching movement. She called on her own experience when she wrote about being multiracial in "Brass Ankles Speak." The mainstream press, dominated by white males, often claimed her work was not marketable due to her controversial stands, and when it was published, she was sometimes not paid for it.

Nevertheless, she persevered, and from around 1920 on, she devoted herself to journalism, writing columns, articles and reviews. She also gave speeches and lectures. Specifically, she wrote "Une Femme Dit" (which began as "From a Woman's Point of View") for the *Pittsburgh Courier* from February 1926 to September 1926. "As in a Looking Glass" appeared in the *Washington Eagle* from 1926 to 1930 and "So It Seems—to Alice Dunbar-Nelson" in the *Courier* from January to May 1930. Through the columns, she worked as a literary critic, political analyst, social commentator, humorist and stage and film critic. Writing in *Opportunity* magazine in "Survey of the Negro Press" in 1917, Eugene Gordon stated, "In my estimation there are few better column conductors of her sex on any newspaper. I should like to see her on some influential daily where her unmistakable talents would be allowed full exercise."

Along the way, Dunbar wrote for a variety of purposes and institutions other than newspapers. From 1913 to 1914, she was co-editor and writer for the *A.M.E. Review*, an influential church publication of the African Methodist Episcopal Church. From 1920, she co-edited the *Wilmington Advocate*, a progressive Black newspaper. She also published the *Dunbar Speaker and Entertainer*, a literary anthology for Black readers.

With the birth of the National Association of Colored Women in 1896 and the subsequent growth of the Black women's club movement, which united to support the development of the race and to erase derogatory stereotypes, Dunbar had ample opportunity to promote her causes. The clubs worked to improve racial treatment in such varied fields as housing, education, civil rights, women's suffrage, travel accommodations, health and cultural affairs. Their accomplishments were impressive, and Dunbar did her part. She organized the National Negro Music Festival in 1929 and helped found organizations such as the Industrial School for Colored Girls in Marshalltown, Delaware, and the White Rose Home for Girls in Manhattan.

In 1914, she published *Masterpieces of Negro Eloquence*, a collection of over five hundred pages filled with fifty-one pieces by forty-five men and four women, all of them focused on the advancement of African Americans. It was dedicated to "the boys and girls of the Negro race…with the hope that it may inspire them with a belief in their own possibilities." She included one of her own essays in the volume: "The Life of Social Service as Exemplified in David Livingstone." It had been delivered originally as a speech at Lincoln University, Pennsylvania, during the centenary of Livingstone's birth in 1913. A hymn of praise to the man, it is inspirational, full of allusions and quotations from literature and history. When *Masterpieces* did not sell, she blamed it on Black readers. As reported by Gloria Hull in *Color, Sex, and Poetry*, she complained in a letter to the noted bibliophile Arthur Schoenburg, "How apathetic is this race of ours—apathetic and pathetically so on literary matters."

In "People of Color in Louisiana," a 1916 essay, Dunbar sought to make the history of people of color in Louisiana more accessible. In 1917, she wrote, "There is no state in the Union, hardly any spot of like size on the globe, where the man of color has lived so intensely, made so much progress, been of such historical importance and yet about which so comparatively little is known."

Politics held a strong attraction for her, and in 1915, she became an organizer for the women's suffrage movement and then, three years later, a field representative in the South for the Women's Committee of the Council on National Defense. In 1920, she became the first Black woman to serve on the State Republican Committee of Delaware. In 1924, she campaigned for the passage of the Dyer Anti-Lynching Bill, which was defeated in Congress by southern Democrats, and she became executive secretary of the American Friends Interracial Peace Committee.

Despite her efforts to improve the lot of African Americans and correct their negative stereotypes, her views on race were complex. She believed that African Americans should have equal access to job opportunities, healthcare and education, but she often made disparaging remarks about the race and even seemed to look down on darker-skinned Blacks, especially if they were less educated. On the other hand, she was an aggressive supporter of Black causes, fighting for justice and equality. She financially aided young women at the Industrial School for Colored Girls. Nevertheless, she seemed to believe that white people were more responsible and efficient than Black people.

Dunbar finished her career by writing detective stories, then a new genre. She often took up what was new and what could bring her income. Beginning with *Violets* and through the early 1900s, her attention was given mostly to her short stories. She considered them her most representative work, and it is primarily the stories for which she is currently remembered. Gloria Hull, in the introduction to *Give Us Each Day*, Dunbar's personal diary, comments, "Her status is secured, foremost, by her short stories, diary, and journalism… and by her prominence as a widely active Black woman during a tumultuous period of American and African-American history."

For a Black woman to keep a diary in the early twentieth century was an unusual practice, but so Dunbar did in 1921 and from 1926 to 1931. When it was finally published in 1984, it was one of only two known journals kept by nineteenth-century African American women in the early twentieth century. As such, it is a valuable window into the lives of Black women during that time. Gloria Hull says that "it may be the most significant and enduring piece of writing that she [Dunbar-Nelson] produced."

The diary addresses issues both personal and global, touching on family, friendships, emotional highs and lows, sexuality, health, travel and day-to-day life. All too often, it records her financial difficulties. (At one point during the Depression, she even thought about selling encyclopedias and Spencer undergarments door to door to get by.) She did not write daily, although she planned to do so, leaving gaps short and long. Nevertheless, it tells the story of what it was to be a Black woman in the early twentieth century. It also fills in gaps in her other writing. Where her essays are full of racial commentary, her writings in what were considered finer genres are nonracial. It is in her diary that we see the whole woman. In it, the real Alice Dunbar emerges. Alice Dunbar-Nelson: wife, poet, teacher, journalist, platform speaker, political activist, stenographer, executive secretary, editor, newspaper columnist and campaign manager. She was indeed a woman of many parts.

Major Works

"As in a Looking Glass" (column for *Washington Eagle* newspaper)
"The Colored United States"
The Dunbar Speaker and Entertainer: Containing the Best Prose and Poetic Selections by and about the Negro Race, with Programs Arranged for Special Entertainments (editor)
"From a Woman's Point of View" (column for *Pittsburgh Courier*)
Give Us Each Day: The Diary of Alice Dunbar-Nelson
The Goodness of St. Roque and Other Stories
"I Sit and I Sew," "Snow in October" and "Sonnet" in *Caroling Dusk: An Anthology of Verse by Negro Poets*, edited by Countee Cullen
Masterpieces of Negro Eloquence: The Best Speeches Delivered by the Negro from the Days of Slavery to the Present Time (editor)
Mine Eyes Have Seen (one-act play)
"People of Color in Louisiana"
"So It Seems to Alice Dunbar-Nelson" (column for *Pittsburgh Courier*)
Various poems published in *Crises*, *Ebony and Topaz* (journal of the NAACP) and *Opportunity* (journal of the Urban League)
Violets and Other Tales
"Wordsworth's Use of Milton's Description of the Building of Pandemonium"

SYBIL KEIN

PRESERVING CRÉOLITÉ

*Kein's poetry has not only aided a Creole renaissance,
but one of celebrating French Louisiana.*
—Mary Morton, "Creole Culture in the Poetry of Sybil Kein"

Sybil Kein (aka Consuela Marie Moore or Consuela Provost) not only follows the professional model established by Alice Dunbar-Nelson; she is one of Dunbar-Nelson's actual descendants. Like her predecessor, Kein is a native New Orleanian who has been a leading promoter of Creole culture, a poet, a scholar and a performer.

Born in New Orleans in 1939, she received her BS degree in viola and violin performance from Xavier University in 1958, her MA in theater arts and communication from Louisiana State University at New Orleans (now University of New Orleans) in 1972 and her DA from the University of Michigan–Ann Arbor in 1975, where she studied with African American poet Robert Hayden while making a comparative study of American ethnic literatures. She has continued to pursue her academic interests throughout her professional career, which has included publication of nine plays, several books on Creole culture and five volumes of poetry. She has also served as a consultant to the McCree Theatre in Genesee County, Michigan.

Those interests are nowhere more evident than in Kein's commitment to promoting all things Creole, from the language as used in New Orleans to its music and its history. Kein conceives of Creole in a broad sense. Her term includes all those, Black and white, of French or Spanish ancestry, who are born in Louisiana and participate in the Creole culture. As she explains in *Gombo People*, surviving Creoles are those "of mixed ethnic makeup who adhere to their inherited rituals, language, social customs and who are native to the state." She uses her skill as a writer, musician, linguist and performer to celebrate and maintain the existence of Créolité.

Kein's writing is one of the principal means of reaching that goal. In "The Use of Louisiana Creole in Southern Literature," she discusses the importance of Creole patois in the literature of the South, the dispersal of contemporary Creoles from South Louisiana to other parts of the country making it all the more important to get narratives into print since the tradition of passing language from one generation to another by oral means is less likely without sizable groups of its speakers. It is their history, language, customs and literature that she works to preserve in belle lettres, songs, stories, games, recipes and more. They make a record of the culture she hopes to sustain.

The cultural attitudes found in her poems often stand in contrast to standard ideas about race. For example, in her explorations into the history, rituals and traditions of Creole culture, she denies the Black-white cultural binary. That denial is evident in her self-identification as African American as well as Creole, and she writes in Creole, French and English, sometimes presenting a poem in French or Creole and following it with the same poem in English. It is also evident in her portrayal of an American South that is different from the one usually depicted in its literature. As Mary Morton points out, Kein creates voices in her writing, both academic and creative, that deny "the romanticized sense of the Old South often found in literature." The fact that she does not adhere to a traditional Black-white social structure or conform to conventional creative traditions has made it harder to put her writing in a particular category. Consequently, it was not until the 1980s and 1990s that she began to receive attention as a notable southern writer.

Kein's poems are varied in subject, voice and purpose. Sometimes she makes linguistic jokes; at other times, she writes lyrics of love. The poems are told in an array of voices: Louisiana Creole, Haitian, Spanish and English. The lyrics of *Gardenias* offer escape from sorrow and pain, but the narratives in *An American South* convey the atrocities of slavery.

In 1981, she published her most popular work, *Gombo People*, a volume of poems, each written first in the Creole language and then translated into English, making it the first original American literature written in Louisiana Creole. As such, it mirrors the earlier publication of *Les Cenelles*, a collection of poems written in French and published in the early nineteenth century. Like its predecessor, it is, according to Kein, totally a Creole effort. She takes pleasure in the fact that all those working on it—the writer, artists, editor and publisher—were Creole.

Her cultural attitudes and support of Creole culture are clearly evident in *An American South* (1996), a collection of poems that she dedicates to friends, African-American scholars and promoters of Créolité. The poems are often built around a real person, group or event. The individual or occurrence may be mentioned in the title, in the poem or in the dedication or the date on which something occurred. For example, in the opening poem of the collection, "1724, La Nouvelle Orleans," she recalls the marriage of Jean Baptiste Raphael and Marie Gaspard at *l'église* of St. Louis in 1724, including their declaration to keep their Creole heritage pure.

Two of the figures who stand out in her poems are Marie Laveau and Marie Thérèse Métoyer, aka Coincoin. The former is featured in "Homage" in *An American South* and in two poems in *Gombo People*. The legend of Marie Laveau is close to Kein's family because a relative of her mother married one of Marie Laveau's children and lived in the Quarter near the Laveau house. In "Homage to Marie Laveau," each stanza is followed by an incantation that recalls the Roman Catholic liturgy and its litanies to Mary. It opens as follows:

> *Isis of the south,*
> *Carrying baskets of*
> *hope, healing salts*
> *from ancient waters, salve for the evil*
> *we do to ourselves.*
>
> *À toi la gloire, et*
> *la paix du Seigneur soit*
> *toujours avec nous.*

Similarly, in "To the Widow Paris" in *Gombo People*, Marie is appealed to, much as a saint would be, to give her people "mystery, hope,/ Courage." In all three poems, she is expected to provide comfort.

The other individual who appears with some frequency in Kein's poems, Marie Thérèse Métoyer, or Coincoin as she was known, is notable for having established a historical community of Creoles of color along the Cane River near Natchitoches, Louisiana. Born a slave, she gained her freedom when Claude Thomas Pierre Métoyer, with whom she had ten children, in addition to five earlier children, purchased it. As a free woman, she manufactured medicine, planted tobacco and trapped wild bears for the sale of their skins in New Orleans. Over time, she amassed large tracts of land and owned slaves, most of whom she bought to save them from other purchasers. After the Civil War, her properties became a settlement for cultured, successful free people of color. Her eldest son, Augustin Métoyer, donated land for a church at Isle Brevelle and in 1829 commissioned his brother Louis to build St. Augustine Parish Church, which is believed to be the first church in America built by free people of color for their own use.

The poem that bears her name in *An American South* opens with these lines:

1786
You were finally free;
and you bought your
children, grandchildren.
And you meant not only freedom,
but land, money.

It ends:

Why do I pick and gouge
frantically at your bones
these Natchitoches
rigolettes? Am I still looking
for my proud grandmother, sister
who is called Marie-Thérèse?
Or does my soul lie grieving
In this fevered mud?

Many of the poems in *An American South* are dark with hurt and loss and remembrances of old injustices. In "Bayou Ballad," for example, the narrator tells the story of Amédé Ardoin's murder. The poem begins and ends with a four-line refrain:

Oh, have you heard
and it was not long ago,
how they killed the sweetest singer
of Cajun zydeco?

On its repetition at the end of the poem, there is a small addition so that it reads:

Oh, have you, have you heard,
and it is not long ago,
how they killed the sweetest singer
of Cajun zydeco? Ahieeeeeeeeeeee!

Other poems in the collection are similarly mournful. "Zalli" is sad, and "Mala," the story of a mother crazed by the sale of her children, is even sadder, but one of the most searing indictments of racism, and of the history of Louisiana as well, is found in the poem the title of which is that of the collection: "An American South," with the subtitle of "Louisiana." It recalls a history of broken promises, political betrayals and insults of all kinds that have threatened the identity and culture of *les gens de couleur.* The opening stanza celebrates the natural beauties of the state:

> *Banana plantains, crepe myrtle*
> *in pink bounty, palmettos*
> *bracing clear sky, mornings*
> *bright with mocking birds*

In contrast, the second stanza states:

> *All this of a spring to cache*
> *memory of chains, bloody hunks*
> *of hair, flesh turned with earth*
> *for planting sweet peas, bodies*
> *of babes wrung limp and plowed*
> *under, eyes, ears, hands rotting*
> *in the sun, genius crushed by law.*

As Mary Morton points out in "Creole Culture in the Poetry of Sybil Kein," "the importance of Kein's poetry cannot be over-estimated, not for the art alone, but for the artistic preservation of Creole history—creating voices of truth that deny the distortions, sentimentalized or not of the tragic mulatto themes found in literature."

Not surprisingly, other elements commonly associated with New Orleans make their way into her writing. There is, obviously, gumbo, a dish that gave its name to her first book of poems, *Gombo People.* It is a natural metaphor for the culture itself that is a mixture of French, Spanish, African, Acadian, Haitian and other peoples who came to Louisiana and joined its rich mixture of backgrounds and beliefs. But food in general is important, too. It, too, gives comfort. But more than that, it is associated with religious practice. In "Nine Rituals," she notes the foods that are appropriate on different saints' days. Four of the nine rites are sanctioned sacraments of the Church, but the others have a sacramental force that comes from the community. (She also writes about New Orleans's food elsewhere.) Needless to say, Mardi Gras makes its appearance in her poetry, too.

Kein's accomplishments go on. Shortly before Katrina hit, Kein completed *Bonjour Créole! Éh la bas! Learn to Speak Louisiana French Creole: An Introduction.* It complements her *Maw-Maw's Creole ABC Book: Pour les Petites for Children.* Both are designed to bring young people into speaking Creole. They also make Louisiana Creole more than just a spoken language by moving it into print. In the field of theater, she is the author of nine produced plays (including a "Historical Revue with Music") and has explored the uses of drama to teach basic subjects in public schools. Her plays, like her poetry, deal with themes of slavery, miscegenation, the color line, the dilemmas of mixed-race Creoles and breaking down stereotypes between whites and Blacks. More recently, she served as editor of *Creole: The History and Legacy of Louisiana's Free People of Color,* in which the first essay is Alice Dunbar-Nelson's "People of Color in Louisiana." In it, Kein connects today's African American achievements to the successes of those who preceded them. Her own essays and presentations range through a variety of New Orleans topics, including jazz funerals, Mardi Gras Indians, Creole music and food culture and African and Afro-Caribbean religions.

In addition to her written efforts to recover the Creole language and to introduce Creole culture to new audiences through her publications, Kein has also reached out through her music. An accomplished musician with, as noted earlier, a degree in music from Xavier of New Orleans, she once auditioned for the New Orleans Symphony Orchestra but was turned down because at that time the orchestra was open to whites only. After experimenting with dance, painting and sculpture, she took up writing, beginning with poetry, which led to the celebration of New Orleans's music in poems to and about Bessie Smith, Ma Rainey and Billie Holiday in *Delta Dancer* (1984), along with other well-researched historical Black and Creole characters, and to recording the songs and poetry of earlier generations of Louisiana Creoles in *Creole Ballads and Zydeco* (1996), *Maw-Maw's Creole Lullaby* (1997) and *Creole Classique* (2000). Her *Sérénade Créole,* a cassette of songs, and its companion text, *Gardenias y Roses,* reflect the Spanish influence on Louisiana Creole music and poetry.

Coming from a musical family, Kein often performs with her daughter and her brothers, who are also active in New Orleans's musical life. Adding her vocals, guitar and percussion to her brother Raymond's classical guitar, banjo and harmonica, they perform as the Creole Troubadours. Together, they exemplify the health and potential of Créolité in Louisiana.

Kein has received numerous honors for her poetry and for her cultural awareness. As the recipient of the Hopwood Award, which has been given by the University of Michigan since 1931, she was honored for both, as it is given for excellence in creative writing, noting in her case that her poetry draws on her Louisiana roots. In addition, she was named Chercheur Associé of the Sorbonne in Paris for her work in Creole culture and as distinguished Professeur Émerité of the University of Michigan. A protégé of Robert Hayden, she is honored by having her poetry housed in the National Archives, Library of Congress.

Clearly Sybil Kein, like Alice Dunbar before her, along with contemporary colleagues such as Elizabeth Brown-Guillory and Brenda Osbey, is a force for cultural preservation. Her poems and her music in particular are the instruments she uses to sustain Creole life. Certainly, her efforts deserve notice and respect.

Major Works

An American South
Creole Ballads
Creole Classique
Creole Journal
Creole: or, The History and Legacy of Louisiana's Free People of Color
Delta Dancer
Gardenias y Rosas: Canciones Romanticas (a musical companion to *Gombo People*)
Gombo People
Love Is Forever: Songs of Romantic New Orleans
Maw Maw's Creole Lullaby and Other Songs for Children
Serenade Creole
Zydeco

PINKIE GORDON LANE

A QUIET PIONEER

*Indeed, her voice is so quiet at times that in the militant 1960s,
hers was not accepted as "African American poetry."*
—*Carolyn M. Jones*

Pinkie Gordon Lane is the quintessential trailblazer. Her list of "firsts"
is long and impressive. She was the first African American woman to
complete a PhD at Louisiana State University. She was the first woman to
serve as chair of the English Department at Southern University. Appointed
by Governor Buddy Roemer, she became Louisiana's first African American
poet laureate. And that's just for starters.

Trailblazing was not easy. Born in Philadelphia, Pennsylvania, in 1923
as the only surviving child of William Alexander Gordon and Inez Addie
West Gordon, Pinkie Gordon Lane grew up in times troubled by racial
strife and the Great Depression. Struggling to provide their daughter with
an education, her parents managed to see her through the prestigious
Philadelphia High School for Girls. After graduation, however, there was
no money for college, and she took a job in a sewing factory. After the death
of both parents, Lane won a four-year scholarship to Spelman College in
Atlanta, Georgia. It was there that she met her husband, Ulysses "Pete"
Simpson. Her degree in English and art from Spelman, where she graduated
with honors, was followed later by a master's degree in English from Atlanta
University and the PhD from LSU.

In the interim between degrees, Lane became an educator, a career she
was to develop for decades to come. She taught high school students in

Georgia and Florida for six years, returning to Atlanta in 1955 to continue her own education. The next year, she accepted a position at Leland College in Baker, Louisiana, where she taught until she moved to join the English Department faculty at Southern University in 1959. Her early years there combined teaching, motherhood and a cross-town commute to LSU to work on her PhD. That experience is recalled in a poem from *Wind Thoughts* titled "While Working towards the PhD Degree":

> *Telephone unanswered, parties unserved,*
> *Husband languishing, flat, unnerved;*
>
> *Friendships neglected, kisses left cold,*
> *Laughter—too much, too sudden, too bold.*
>
> *Tears—much too quickly, as quickly forgot,*
> *A child loved and wanted, but with prudence ungot*
>
> *Dust on the table, a kitten unmilked.*
> *Love but indulged, flowing loosely like silk.*
>
> *Ethereally lost in the cold world of print,*
> *A drunken desire, incontinent,*
>
> *Ideas my only reality,*
> *A slave in pursuit of that damned Ph.D.*

With the PhD and time, Lane became department chair of English, and her husband taught in the Department of Education. When he died of lung and liver cancer in 1970, Lane continued to develop as a scholar, poet and single mother at Southern, where she spent the rest of her career. Her devotion to art and beauty, despite the disappointments and banalities of life, never wavered, as reflected in "On Being Head of the English Department":

> *I will look with detachment*
> *On the signing of contracts*
> *the ordering of books,*
> *and the making of schedules—*
> *will sing hymns of praise*
> *to the negative, when*
> *it is necessary to survive.*

And if the morning
light freezes in the east,
a dawn-covered eye
will tell me I am cold
to your pleas, but never whore
to the spirit. I will
write poems in the blue-frosted lake.

If I disdain poetasters,
announcers, and the gods
of mediocrity, knowing
that they too insist on living,
it is because I hand you
the bread and the knife
but never the music and the art
of my existence.

You will not swallow me or absorb me:
I have grown too lean for that.
I am selfish, I am cruel.

I am love.

In addition to her teaching, Lane planned to write short stories. That is, she planned to work with fiction until 1962, when, on the recommendation of a friend, she found *A Street in Bronzeville* by Gwendolyn Brooks. Reading a book of poetry by a Black woman was a life-changing experience, causing Lane to turn to poetry as her genre of choice. That a single book could cause such a transformative experience might seem surprising today, but it must be remembered that Black studies courses were in their infancy in the early '60s, and scholarship surrounding Black artists was rare, making such a discovery a powerful one.

Nevertheless, it was not until 1972 that Lane published *Wind Thoughts*, her first book of poetry. It was well received but did not get the notice that her second book, *The Mystic Female*, elicited in 1978. A year after its publication, Gwendolyn Brooks nominated it for the Pulitzer Prize. It was followed by three more books of poetry: *I Never Scream* (1985), *Girl at the Window* (1991) and *Elegy for Etheridge* (2000).

Lane's poetry entered the world at a tumultuous time for writers and readers. With the struggle for civil rights in full swing, much of the art and letters produced by Black artists of the time was full of anger and venom. Lane's was not. Instead, her voice was quiet. Notably, she titled her third book of poetry *I Never Scream*. The contrast between her work and that of other Black writers was not missed, resulting in criticism from colleagues and members of the Black Arts Movement for not falling in line with what they deemed to be authentic Black poetry. It was not Black enough for them; that is, it lacked the relevant Black themes they felt with such urgency. Carolyn M. Jones described Lane's work as follows: "Indeed, her voice is so quiet at times that in the militant 1960s, hers was not accepted as 'African American poetry.'" Kelly Harris says that Margaret Ambrose, a friend and colleague at Southern, explained, "Pinkie didn't want to be known as a Black poet, but simply as a poet. It was important to her that she write about her racial experiences and beyond it. She wanted to reach a universal audience, and her poems did reach across racial lines at the time." Jones reports that Dudley Randall of Broadside Press finally called Lane's work "another kind of Black poetry, balancing intimacy with emotion with interpretive distance."

In a 1990 interview with Danella P. Hero for *Louisiana Literature*, Lane recalled confiding in the poet, editor and activist Margaret Danner about the criticism: "I am getting a lot of rejection from these people who say I should be writing about Black issues and 'throw your Molotov cocktail at whitey' and all this kind of thing, but that's not the kind of poetry I write. [Danner] said, 'You go right on being yourself. We all have to develop our own audience.' I needed to hear that" (quoted in *64 Parishes*). And apparently, Lane took the advice to heart, as she continued to produce poems that were true to herself and her style.

"A Quiet Poem," from *I Never Scream: New and Selected Poems* (1985), explains her stance:

> *This is a quiet poem.*
> *Black people don't write*
> *many quiet poems*
> *because what we feel*
> *is not a quiet hurt.*
> *And a not quiet hurt*
> *does not call for muted tones.*
>
> *But I will write a poem*
> *about this evening*

full of the sounds
of small animals, some fluttering
in thick leaves, a smear
of color here and there—
about the whispers of darkness
a gray wilderness of light
descending, touching
breathing.

I will write a quiet poem
immersed in shadows
and mauve colors
and spots of white
fading into deep tones
of blue.

This is a quiet evening
full of hushed singing
and light that has no
ends, no breaking
of the planes, or brambles
thrusting out.

Lane's contribution to the cause of Black artists was in no way lacking, however. It was, in fact, deeply significant. When Melvin Butler, founder of the Southern University Black Poetry Festival, died suddenly, Lane, along with Charles Rowell, founder of the well-known literary journal *Callaloo*, assumed the job of coordinating the festival. Under their leadership, it became a means for Black artists—writers, as well as those working in jazz, visual arts and theater—to both celebrate their culture and sharpen their skills. It gave them a way to find their own community.

In time, the festival gained a national reputation, by the mid-1970s attracting such talent as Lucille Clifton and Audre Lorde. Keynote speakers featured luminaries such as Hoyt Fuller, one-time editor of *Negro Digest*, and Toni Morrison. Interestingly, Morrison's appearance was in 1977, eleven years before she won a Pulitzer Prize. Dr. Jerry Ward, retired professor from Tougaloo and Dillard University, called the festival "destination: blackness." Eventually, with Lane's support, the name of the festival was changed to the Melvin Butler Poetry Festival in honor of its founder.

Lane took a very public avenue to deal with another issue of Black equality when, in 1990, she wrote a letter to the *Baton Rouge Advocate* responding to an article Rod Dreher had published titled "Writers Find Baton Rouge a Good Place to Live and Write." As she pointed out in her letter, he failed to profile a single Black writer in his article. As she said (and was quoted in *64 Parishes*), "We [Black poets] are also Baton Rouge writers. Or don't we count?" But equal treatment for race was not the only cause she championed. Like the modern woman that she was, she also fought against misogyny, arguing for the empowerment and equity of women.

Despite the fact that she was never popular with her contemporary Black artists, those who considered her work "not Black enough," the widespread readership she found in journals, anthologies and her own books offered her prizes aplenty. In 1989, she was appointed poet laureate of Louisiana by Governor Buddy Roemer. For three years, she fulfilled the duties of that post, including representing the state in the 1996 Olympic torch relay—the first African American to do so. Her second book of poems, *The Mystic Female*, was nominated for a Pulitzer Prize, and her work gained notice beyond that of only book lovers when music director and conductor Dinos Constantinides wrote *Listenings and Silences*, classical compositions based on her poems. An even broader audience was introduced to her work by the film *Love Jones*, a romantic comedy that featured an all-Black cast. At a high point in the movie, Lane's poem "I Am Looking at Music," from *Girl at the Window*, was recited, making it a piece of performative art.

It is the color of light,
the shape of sound high in the evergreens
It lies suspended in hills,
A blue line in a red sky.

I am looking at sound.

I am hearing the brightness
Of high bluffs and almond trees
I am tasting the wilderness
of lakes, rivers, and streams
Caught in an angle of song
I am remembering water
that glows in the dawn
The motion tumbled in earth

Life hidden in mounds.
I am dancing a bright beam of light

I am remembering love.

Today, Pinkie Gordon Lane is widely remembered by those who enjoy her poetry, but she is celebrated nowhere more than in Baton Rouge, where both LSU and Southern University honor her memory. The former holds an annual Pinkie Gordon Lane Poetry Contest open to students from throughout the state. The winners are celebrated on campus at an awards program and reception. At the latter institution, a group of students dedicated to fighting against racism petitioned the university to rename the John W. Parker Agricultural Coliseum, which honored a former governor who is said to have been a racist who participated in the lynching of Sicilian immigrants. The students asked that his name be replaced by that of Pinkie Gordon Lane. It is a fitting tribute to a poet who never screamed but fought her own quiet and powerful fight.

Major Works

Elegy for Etheridge
Girl at the Window
I Never Scream
The Mystic Female
Wind Thoughts

BRENDA MARIE OSBEY

CAPTURING A CULTURE IN POETRY

The mission of the poet as historian/geographer is to trace
the cultural terrain of a place and a people.
—Violet Harrington Bryan

Another native New Orleanian whose writing is marked by her birthplace is Brenda Marie Osbey. In her poetry, the city is a major player, serving as both backdrop and subject, which reflects her description of her work as "a kind of cultural biography and cultural geography." As she explained to Andrea Rushing, "I write about New Orleans, what makes it the way it is—the way we talk, the way we think, the way we live."

Born in 1957, Osbey was educated at Dillard University, Paul Valéry University and the University of Kentucky and has gone on to teach at UCLA, Loyola University in New Orleans and Dillard. She has served as visiting writer in residence at Tulane and scholar in residence at Southern University. She is currently distinguished visiting professor of Africana studies at Brown University. Osbey is not solely a teacher, however. She is also the author of poetry, prose and nonfiction, written in both English and French. She is also interested in the poetry of the pre-colonial and colonial eras. And there is always the appeal of New Orleans, its culture and its history.

Her fascination with and knowledge of the city have earned her a multitude of honors. She served as the first peer-selected poet laureate of Louisiana from 2005 to 2007. She has received fellowships and awards from the National Endowment for the Arts, the Louisiana Division of the

Arts and the New Orleans Jazz and Heritage Foundation. In 1998, she was given the American Book Award for *All Saints*; in 1984, she received the Associated Writing Programs Poetry Award; and in 2014, she received the Langston Hughes Award for Poetry from the College Language Association. She has also been awarded the Louisiana Board of Regents Award to Artists and Scholars, the Louisiana Writers Foundation Award for Excellence in Poetry and the Academy of American Poets Loring-Williams Award. She has been a resident at the MacDowell Colony, the Fine Arts Work Center in Provincetown, Millay Colony, the Kentucky Foundation for Women, Virginia Center for the Creative Arts, the Fine Art Works Center in Philadelphia, the Bunting Institute of Radcliffe College, Harvard University and at Cassis, France, courtesy of a Camargo Foundation Fellowship.

Osbey is drawn to New Orleans for a number of reasons. For one, she values its ethnic diversity made up of people who retain their family heritage and at the same time are touched by the city's unique ambiance. "People cling to their ethnicity [in New Orleans,] and even flaunt it!" In an interview with John Lowe, she asserted that New Orleans has been primarily influenced by African culture, calling it "a distinctly black space" with "whites as marginal." One of its strengths, she continued, is that it has managed to take in so many cultures. She also values that, like much of the South in general, it tends to hold on to what is old and historic, to be comfortable with its past. It does not forget family, living and dead, along with their codes of behavior.

Religion she sees as equally diverse in the city. Hoodoo, she says, is the dominant religion in New Orleans, despite the Catholicism of the Spanish and French. (Voodoo is known as Hoodoo in New Orleans.) As she explained in that same interview with John Lowe, "The spirituality here is uniquely African in nature." The African religions that slaves knew (and brought with them) have powerful, sensual, sexual female deities worshiped by women and men. They are neither pious nor celibate nor subordinate to male deities. She continues: "And then there's a kind of Protestantism that is peculiar to New Orleans as well; we have the early Spiritual Sanctified churches here, which Spiritual and Sanctified people will tell you do not grow out of Hoodoo, but all of the evidence is that they did. But the nature of religion in New Orleans is really very bizarre….One of the things that Catholicism does to New Orleans is that it allows for coexistence of all kinds of seeming opposites." Even the sacred and secular function side by side. The result is "a kind of peaceful coexistence among institutions and people, and among ideas and among cultures." She cites as an example a bar with an exit in back of one of the oldest churches in the city, so that when mass starts, the barkeeper unplugs the jukebox. In the same way, she sees her own work as cutting across the boundaries of secular and sacred experience.

Then there are the specific places she is drawn to in New Orleans, one of them being its cemeteries, those cities of the dead that are connected to the living city with its built environments, its streets and houses. The two exist side by side in a complex interface of the living and the dead that provides the basis of many of her poems that invoke the ancestral dead "to continue to live among us" and call to the newly dead to come home to the community.

Osbey's abiding interest in New Orleans led her to a study of West African, Caribbean and French cultural traditions, practices and beliefs that interconnect there and inevitably find their way into her poetry and essays in a way that creates a spiritual sense of the city. As she told Lowe, "New Orleans is definitely the spiritual core of everything I write." She is uniquely qualified for such work, as she is fluent in French (and speaks other languages), has traveled widely and spent years in archival work in the New Orleans Public Library as assistant director of the Foreign Languages Division, then moved to the Louisiana Division, working mainly in the New Orleans Archives. When such interests appear in articles she has done for the *New Orleans Tribune* or her Tremé poems or early essays, the reader is pushed to reconsider the dead and rethink how history was made. Thus, she has blended her deep roots in Creole culture with a wider world outlook.

Her poems do not always make for easy reading. They tell stories, often long stories. (The writers Robert Hayden, Jay Wright and Gwendolyn Brooks have been helpful to Osbey, as they, too, favor the genre.) The level of difficulty is increased as Osbey assumes that the reader understands local vocabularies, artifacts and practices. For those who don't, she often provides a glossary of New Orleans ethnic expressions, place names and characters.

Osbey tells stories, but not in an orderly fashion. They rarely have a beginning, middle and end. More important than the stories themselves, perhaps, are the ways they are told or the characters who tell them, as they seem to be a way of speaking or thinking. She often has several characters develop the narrative from different perspectives, or individual characters may tell the story from several of their own viewpoints. (The different voices telling their stories have sometimes led to comparisons with Edgar Lee Masters's *Spoon River Anthology*.) That means that one character may tell different versions or speak in different voices. The narrator may change from time to time without signposts for the reader, making the language the cue that another character has entered the conversation. "Ceremony for Minneconjoux," for example, begins in unidentified third person and then moves to Mama Lou's daughter, Lenazette. It ends with the speaker being Minneconjoux, Lenazette's daughter. These techniques are the result of her choice to write what Osbey calls a "community of narrative" or "narratives of community." Her explanation, as reported by Violet Bryan in the *Mississippi Quarterly*, was: "The concept I build is a literal community in which people live. I see narrative as a kind of community—the talking to and the talking about or through."

Writing in free verse, Osbey uses irregular line length and disregards conventional punctuation and capitalization. The style is primarily expository, tweaked by her inventive use of line, stanza and phrase. The community emerges from her allusions to the history, folklore, rituals and geography of New Orleans. The references to a home on Bayou Lafourche and St. Claude Street, for example, ground the actions of a poem in a particular place. It is a style that, according to Calvin C. Hernton, produces stories that "aspire… to the condition of myth."

It is not only the places and practices of the city that attract Osbey's interest. People catch her eye and ear as well. Those who make it into her poems are drawn from New Orleans's diverse population, some of them from local history, and others who may seem ordinary on the outside prove to be quite the opposite.

To say that the characters that appear in her narrative poems, many of them women, are colorful is an understatement. They are three-dimensional, revealing their inner selves, which are often violent and disruptive, eccentric and sensual. Ironically, they become individualized through their resistance to the strict social rules they live under, although at the same time they adhere to the rituals and ceremonies of Louisiana culture. Their resistance makes them more than stereotypes, and they often end in madness or death. Osbey does not explain them or judge them, but they stay in memory well after the poem ends.

The peculiar language they speak is full of poetic devices along with Creole words that require the reader to use the glossary that Osbey usually provides. Many of her poems are performances by characters, reminiscent of the performances in Congo Square. Like much that is unique about the city, she says she doesn't think her characters could exist anywhere else.

Many of the poems in her first four published volumes—*Ceremony for Minneconjoux* (1983), *In These Houses* (1988), *Desperate Circumstance, Dangerous Woman* (1991) and *All Saints: New and Selected Poems* (1997)—are peopled by women, along with their spouses and family members, who defy social norms. In *Ceremony for Minneconjoux* and *In These Houses*, there are women whose lives have endured spiritual crises and love affairs gone wrong. And always there is the struggle to live in a modern environment that does not coexist comfortably with the traditions and rituals of the African American community. The characters and their situations incorporate the folklore that produces the uniqueness of the city. Together, they re-create a Louisiana of the past, particularly that of urban New Orleans in the first half of the last century.

"Ceremony for Minneconjoux" has many of the characteristics typically found in Osbey's poems. It is a tale that touches on social structures, language, history, rituals and geography, all of them rooted in New Orleans and surrounding territory. Osbey's research while working in the New Orleans Archives became the groundwork for much of this poem and those of *In These Houses*.

The narrative interest in "Minneconjoux" lies predominantly in the rigid social structure the women of the poem find themselves in and the madness and violence it produces. The women go along with many of the ceremonies and rituals, but they also protest, in any way possible, against the elements of the strict social structure. When Lenazette kills her husband, for instance, she is deemed insane, but in her own way, she is making a protest against the restrictions she lives under in an effort to establish her own identity. It is the story of the madness that comes out of Black lives lived in a racially defined society.

It is also full of allusions to Louisiana folk traditions. There is, for example, the Indian's ritual of combing Lenazette's hair, an expression of sexual interest in a young woman. Some of the ceremonies it depicts, such as the traditional appearance of the Indians in the Mardi Gras parades, recall practices that grew out of the early history of African slaves who escaped to live with Indian tribes, often intermarrying. In 1880, with the advent of the modern Carnival (parades, masks, etc.), a group of young Black people dressed as Indians and joined in. The leaders, or First Chiefs, were either Native Americans or their descendants who carried on the rituals of the ancient Native American and African American traditions. They sang, danced and drummed and created their fantastical costumes following rituals that held the tribal organizations together. The revelers even today are African Americans, Native Americans or their descendants who, costumed in extraordinarily elaborate costumes, sing and dance and drum to reenact their people's ancient practices that are a binding force not only among its members, but also a binding force to the past.

The poems of Osbey's second collection, *In These Houses*, like *Ceremony for Minneconjoux*, grew out of her work in the New Orleans Archives that allowed her to write about the various histories of New Orleans. The poems are divided into three groups: "Houses of the Swift Easy Women," "House of Mercies" and "House of Bones," each representing some part of the history of the city's life and environment: shared, personal and spiritual. The house in Osbey's poems is communal and private, domestic and public. It also connects the past with the present.

Nowhere is the long narrative poem more fully developed than in *Desperate Circumstance, Dangerous Woman*, Osbey's third volume. It is a single poem divided into twelve chapters that tell the story of Marie Crying Eagle and her relationships with family members and her lover, Percy, a troubled situation that leads them to Ms. Regina, a family friend who is a conjurer. It is one fairly lengthy story with several minor narratives embedded in it. Told against the backdrop of Tremé, a New Orleans district originally settled by free Blacks in the 1710s and 1720s, it features mysterious Hoodoo practices, particularly those that have come from the Caribbean. The story is full of the expected magic, exoticism and eroticism. It incorporates Creole speech, Hoodoo practices and exotic characters, creating a haunting sense of place. It remembers the city, the slave past and the vodoun's work.

Part II shifts to the Faubourg, another old section of the city that is highly African and ritualistic. Its traditional reverence for the dead, who are recognized as a living presence, reflects the traditions of the Latin and African cultures there. The acceptance of the existence of the dead among the living culminates in an annual ritual that relates to today's observance of All Saints' Day.

Like the feast day of its title, "All Saints" honors the dead. In twenty narrative poems, it recalls varied historical figures such as Juan San Malo, leader of a slave rebellion, as well as ancestors familial and spiritual. The narrator talks with them, listens to them, walks with them. The dead surround the living at every turn.

The upshot is a mystical spell in which the dead live in the slave-bricked streets, in the images of saints, in Hoodoo rites and in those who "walk upon the earth a living man / wearing all the shrouds of mourning like a skin / and memory like a stone inside your organs" ("Another Time and Farther South"). The reader hears a multitude of voices drawn from colonial times onward. One hears a dialogue with Mother Catherine, a Hoodoo woman and healer; reads a letter to Nina Simone called "The Evening News"; and meets myriad brothers and sisters, crazed women, even the "thrumming city itself." The focus on memory and on death is apparent at the opening invocation. Osbey writes:

*The slave ancestors who lie beneath the swamps, inside the
brick of which our
homes, our streets, our churches are made;
who wrought iron into vévés that hold together the Old
City and its attachments;
personal gods and ancestors; musicians and street dancers;
Hoodoo saints and their little Catholic cousins…
our saints continue to live among us.*

May they never leave us.
May the newly sanctified find their way home to us also.
May they feed well and be pleased with these offerings.
And soon
One day
May we all be counted among them.

The first section of the book, "Live Among Your Dead, Whom You Have Every Right to Love," has several elegies that develop the themes of death and memory. A narrative poem about a lifelong affair, "Desire and Private Griefs," continues the focus in a different poetic form. The final poem in this section, "Peculiar Fascination with the Dead," provides insight into Osbey's contemplation of death and memory. It has the sound of personal practice stemming from personal beliefs. It opens with instructions for how to honor the dead and then turns to a story of a childhood experience in a cemetery that involves finding a skull, subsequently moves through family reminiscences and ends with a catalog of personal practices regarding the dead.

Part II, "In the Faubourg," is set in the Faubourg Tremé and the Faubourg Marigny. The former is the oldest African American neighborhood in the United States. Its heart is Congo Square, giving it a revered place in the history of the Diaspora. Osbey's familiarity with the area's past due to her years of research into the city archives is again evident here. (She also wrote a series of articles about it for the *New Orleans Tribune*, then some Tremé poems and finally essays on the subject.) Her knowledge allows her to place the stories of its people in an accurate historical context. More specifically, it allows her to re-create the district's long association with Creoles of color, its connections with slavery and the economic struggles of its women.

Part III, "Ex Votos," meaning "an offering," is composed of historical vignettes from the past such as "The Head of Luis Congo Speaks." Other poems such as "St. Martin" pay tribute to the saints of the Catholic Church, some real, some false. Several reference places that have seen Black suffering. "Sor Juana," for example, set in Lima, Peru, tells, in English sprinkled throughout with Spanish, the story of a wild and holy woman who was stoned and died cursing her executioners. Finally, "Suicide City," the last poem in this section, is Osbey's long and powerful personal offering to the city.

The final part of *All Saints* indicates the direction Osbey was moving. The practice of portraying experiences of historical figures against a backdrop of actual historical events is continued in *History and Other Poems*. Another connection is that the poems in both show the link between modern culture and that of Africa along with connections between past events and current history.

All Souls: Essential Poems is a collection of pieces drawn from earlier publications. Since the publisher of *History and Other Poems* went out of business, its poems are reprinted in *All Souls* along with some earlier poems that deal with Diasporan history. They contradict the romanticized images and stories of the slave trade with references to images and places connected to it. They speak of the pain that came with the conquest of the New World: contagion, the Middle Passage and slave labor.

Osbey has written several "stand-alone" poems of note. She was, for example, asked to write a poem commemorating the fiftieth anniversary of the integration of the College of William and Mary, which led to commemorative poems for the University of Virginia, including the university's involvement with slavery. In the fall of 2018, she took a position with the Virginia Foundation for the Humanities as the Emilia Galli Struppa Fellow. The result is a narrative historical poem sequence, *Virginia Suite*, which examines the interactions of Africans, Native Americans and Europeans in the early years of the Virginia Colony. In a larger sense, it looks at Virginia's role in the exploration, settlement and shaping of America.

Another stand-alone poem that received considerable notice is "On Contemplating the Breasts of Pauline Lumumba." In January 1961, Patrice Lumumba, the first prime minister of the Republic of Congo, was assassinated. In response, his wife made her grief public by walking bare-breasted through the streets of Leopoldville. The poem honors not only her personal mourning and her protest at the death of her husband but also the combined joy of achieving independence and grieving the loss of a leader.

Although she is best known and widely honored for her poems, Osbey has had success in other genres as well. After her essay "I Want to Die in New Orleans" was published, she became well known, and admired, for her work in that form. She also appeared in a 2008 documentary, *Faubourg Tremé: The Untold Story of Black New Orleans*.

Andrea B. Rushing calls Osbey "the consummate New Orleans poet." And so she is with her focus on memory, the melding of cultures and regions and rituals and the presence of death in life. Yet she is more. Her vision grows out of the city but reaches beyond it to comment on injustice, passion and suffering. She may be a New Orleans poet, but she touches the universal as well.

Major Works

Books

All Saints: New and Selected Poems
Ceremony for Minneconjoux
Desperate Circumstances, Dangerous Woman
In These Houses

Anthologies

Andrews, William L., ed. *Literature of the American South: A Norton Anthology. New York: W.W. Norton and Co., 1997.*

Piercy, Marge, ed. *Early Ripening: American Women's Poetry Now*. Kitchen, Canada: Pandora Press, 1988.

Rowell, Charles H., ed. *Making Callaloo: 25 Years of Black Literature*. New York: St. Martin's Press, 2014.

Smock, Frederick, ed. *The American Voice Anthology of Poetry*. Lexington: University of Kentucky Press, 1998.

Stokesbury, Leon, ed. *The Made Thing: An Anthology of Contemporary Southern Poetry*. Fayetteville: University of Arkansas Press, 1999. 2nd ed.

MONA LISA SALOY

FOLKLORIST AND POET

*Mona Lisa Saloy's poems are love songs to family and freedom
and the magic of the city that continues to define her work and her life.*
—Pearl Cleage

Like several other poets examined here, Mona Lisa Saloy has been hailed as the quintessential New Orleans poet, but she differs from some of her contemporaries who write of the city's painful past, its exoticism and mysterious ambiance. In contrast, Saloy records everyday events in the lives of her Black community, even the smallest of ordinary pleasures: a child jumping rope, her father's pleasure in his early morning "coffee with chicory in his cream and sugar," the sounds of a New Orleans night or what she refers to as "shotgun life." Even "The Ballad of Marie Laveau," her account of the Voodoo practitioner's life and subsequent veneration, has a playfulness to it.

Saloy's keen sense of observation is not surprising since she is not only a poet but also a folklorist, a training that has sharpened her sense of life as it happens and enables her to re-create it in her poems. The details of the lives around her, the relationships of family and friends, their everyday talk and activities, singing in the church choir, the African American roots of her community—all are part of the portrait she paints of her city.

Born shortly after her mother had a fainting spell (or was visited by a "haint"), she was named Mona Lisa by her father. The name had been made popular at the time by a song sung by Nat King Cole. (Her uncles sang it to her when she was a child, leading her to think it was written just for her.) Born into a family of five children in the Seventh Ward in New Orleans, she recalls, "I was loved by hard-working parents, siblings, aunts, uncles, grandparents on both sides, then massive cousins, even more neighbors, who shared backyard meals with us and we with them." Her mother, whom she describes as "the family rock," was lost to cancer soon after Saloy turned sixteen.

Her father was a master carpenter who loved reading and writing for his own pleasure. After serving with a Black unit in World War II, where he continued his carpentry, he began working for the U.S. Army Transportational Terminal Command Gulf, and after turning down an offer to move with the company to the West Coast (for who would ever want to leave New Orleans?), he built shipping boxes for new propellers of oceangoing vessels for Edward's Engineering. After his retirement, he applied his skills to neighborhood repairs and refurbishment. As Saloy remembers it, "The women made red beans and rice, maybe with Gailet, pan-fried shortening bread, when there was no money for French bread; and all the men, they shared their skills: plumbing, electrical, carpentry, all of which were illegal for Blacks who were kept out of unions." It was a *coup de main*: all hands together.

As a child, Saloy spent summers swimming at Hardin Park and school terms skating on weekends at Corpus Christi gym, attending the Circle Show, where she sat in the colored-only balcony for twenty-five cents and shared popcorn if she and her friends had saved their nickels. She dreamed of becoming a champion swimmer or a fashion designer. Instead, she moved to the Northwest, where she earned a BA from the University of Washington–Seattle and an MA from San Francisco State. "My sister made me go to college," she said. "I took to it like a fish to water—or, as we would say, like a crawfish to mud." While there, she was in a car accident that took her memory with it. Encouraged by writers she met at a coffee shop, she "wrote to remember," as she told Judy Christy.

Saloy stresses the importance of the oral tradition in folklore, praising her grandfather, "a great storyteller," for helping her learn her art. The practice became somewhat of a family tradition as her father, with only a third-grade education, wrote all his life, whatever was needed for those who could not do it for themselves: letters, Social Security forms, job applications, eulogies. He even published a poem titled "the Sea" in the army journal. Following his pattern, she prepared herself to be a writer by returning from her time in the Northwest to Louisiana to earn an MFA in creative writing and a PhD in English from Louisiana State University. Currently she serves as the coordinator of English and the Conrad N. Hilton Endowed Professor of English at Dillard University, where she is also the founding director of the Creative Writing Program. One of her highest honors came in the spring of 2021, when she was named poet laureate of Louisiana, giving her the opportunity to travel the state to share her work with fans new and old.

Her teaching and professional involvements extend beyond the walls of the traditional classroom. She is a longtime participant in the Louisiana Endowment for the Humanities–sponsored Prime Time Family Reading Time Programs, a family literacy program designed for children ages three through ten and their families. She is also an active member of the Louisiana Folklore Society and a noted speaker and storyteller.

Saloy writes in numerous genres. As a folklorist, she is interested in the importance of play, documenting sidewalk songs, jump-rope rhymes and clap-hand games, many of which she herself played as a child. She has written on the significance of the Black Beat poets, the African American Toasting Tradition and Black and Creole talk. In addition to numerous articles and reviews, some of which are available online at the Louisiana Division of the Arts Folklife website, her screenplay *Rocking for a Risen Savior*, based on material by Joyce Marie Jackson, director of African American Studies at LSU, premiered in Paris in 2016. The National Constitution Center in Philadelphia commissioned her to compose and perform a poem titled "We," the most important word in the United States Constitution, celebrating Liberty Medal recipients President William J. Clinton and President George H.W. Bush. The poem was later published in *Konch*, an online journal, and is included in *Second Line Home*.

Despite her success in these various genres, it is her poetry that has attracted the most notice. Her collection titled *Red Beans and Ricely Yours* was the winner of the T.S. Eliot Prize in Poetry in 2005 and the PEN/Oakland Miles Prize in 2006. It could be called a hymn to Black New Orleans, as it celebrates the day-to-day lives of Black New Orleanians, whose cultural roots reach back in time. Using street idioms and alluding to personal as well as local history and color, the poems speak lovingly of a culture all its own. As Ishmael Reed, 2005 T.S. Eliot Prize judge, commented, "These poems are music to the ear as well as on the page."

The opening stanza of the first poem in the collection, "Word Works," introduces what is to follow:

I'm about how words
work up a gumbo of culture,
stamped and certified African,
delivered on southern American soil.
In my word house,
we spit out articles and prepositions
like bitter chewing tobacco.
We lean on words that paint pictures of galait
and grits and good times,
sittin' under gallery shades,
sippin' lemonade,
wearin' the afternoon
like a new dress.

The poems that follow introduce the reader to family members, neighborhood life, love, southern life, Black history and more. The collection ends on an optimistic note with a poem titled "We've Come This Far," the concluding stanzas of which state:

Because God called,
Negroes answered as Christian soldiers,
Blacks took to Jesus like a crawfish to mud.
God is no stranger in our homes.
We are soldiers at war under divine charge,
prayer the only down payment,
faith the daily deposit.

Whatever the cost of time
God paid in death to jim crow, integration,
rights, civil rights,
affirmative selves furnished each generation,
At least for those about the Lord's business.
The constant cost, a listening heart,
to the Greatest Voice to echo.

So we rap to the Lord regularly,
consult on corners at church,
and in the quiet of a look.

We've come this far by faith.

For her next book, Saloy chose to reference a popular New Orleans tradition by calling it *Second Line Home: New Orleans Poems.* In a recent article in *64 Parishes*, Matt Sakakeeny explained the makeup of the famous "second line" in New Orleans funeral parades. He wrote:

> *The musicians, funeral directors, family, and friends of the dead make up what is called the first or main line, while the crowd marching behind is collectively known as the second line. As the procession moves from the funeral service to the burial site, the first and second lines march to the beat of a brass band. At the beginning, the band plays dirges, somber Christian hymns performed at a slow walking tempo. After the body is laid to rest, or "cut loose," the band starts playing up-tempo music, the second liners begin dancing, and the funeral transforms into a street celebration.*

Published in 2014, *Second Line Home* recalls Hurricane Katrina in particular and hurricanes in general. Saloy recalls the fearful anticipation of the approach; the darkness of the landing; the heat, stench and effort to clean and rebuild that followed. The poems are both personal and communal. They speak of her personal loss, which was most everything, including her home in the Seventh Ward, and the city's devastation. Both her life and that of the city eventually came full circle. After fifteen moves to three states and five cities, she made it back home, and after a time, the strength and resilience of the city returned it to life. Each stage of the experience is celebrated in the poems. They proclaim that in the darkest of moments, there is family and faith and music to sustain the body and spirit. In the end, joy replaces despair. The Second Line turns sorrow into a celebration. Tony Belden calls *Second Line Home* "a haunting poetic narrative of the horror of Hurricane Katrina and an uplifting, healing song of personal and collective resilience."

In a stanza from "September 2005, New Orleans," Saloy depicts the devastated city. She writes:

> *Once in the neighborhood, the smell of death*
> *Laced streets, covered in debris, along the sidewalks,*
> *Enough room to pass, with some live wires popping,*
> *No sign of anything alive, no birds chirping, no*
> *'squitoes buzzing, no cats crossing, no dogs running.*
> *No people here, downtown, or cars either, just empty*
> *Silence, so loud, like the dead ghost towns of the old West.*

Then, in "New Orleans, Broken Not Dead," she pictures the city's recovery:

If we must break and lose our land to them
Hunted and penned in an inglorious dome,
From signs and lies and tales too tall to find
Making their mock at our drowned homes
While round us each to sweep to dig to build
With wood with brick with steel so strong and clean
Our culture food our dance we love to live
Though first outnumbered, we ache we show us brave
Our craftsmen carve and pour our iron our wood
In vain for months we search our loves our lost
Then build one wall one floor one door one roof
The stench the dead so long in heat with us
Like men and women, bold, we make our pact,
Pressed to our knees, held down but kicking back!

The poems in *Second Line Home* are notable for their authenticity. The language is true to New Orleans speech, using local expressions from the city's streets and picturing down-home activities that any reader will recognize. Typical is "December 2005 at Stephanie's House." The fourth stanza follows:

We half-sit, half-stand
In Stephanie and Warren's kitchen,
Our lives then, what we knew like backyard Sunday brunches,
Our eyes stare, our minds blank.
We hug tight, we rejoice
We again, after months gone
Our once-beautiful homes, memories now:
Connie's dad—Mush's Halloween b-day bashes
With gumbo, bus-stop line dances
Old-school swinging to Smokey Robinson
Fundraisers for St. Raymond Church
Or a bridal shower for a daughter, a cousin
The lovely yard soaked now in the stench of death.
One family at a time, returning
To find out what's left.

Mona Lisa Saloy's talents are many and her energies vast, ranging from teaching to folklore to performances and talks, articles and poems. Her following grows as her publications increase. What will come next? All we can count on is her comment that she writes for those who don't, or can't, speak for themselves. And for the rest of us, too, we hope.

Major Works

Between Laughter and Tears: Black Mona Lisa Poems
Red Beans and Ricely Yours
Second Line Home: New Orleans Poems

ELIZABETH BROWN-GUILLORY

SCHOLAR, TEACHER, PLAYWRIGHT

In my writing, I choose to write about Louisiana and its gumbo people
because my home state shaped my view of the world,
namely that it is important to see people for who they are
and to accept and embrace both the similarities and differences.
—Elizabeth Brown-Guillory

Church Point is a small town in Southwest Louisiana. It is chiefly known for being the home of Iry Lejeune (who brought the accordion back into Cajun music after World War II), Jean Horecky (the first Yambilee Queen) and Zydeco musicians BooZoo Chavis and Chubby Carrier. Some would say it is a fairly typical Cajun village. To the casual visitor, it is notable for its family crawfish boils, daily masses at Our Lady of the Sacred Heart Church and the quiet lives led there. According to Elizabeth Brown-Guillory, however, it has produced some characters who are anything but ordinary, and they populate her plays to the delight of audiences who have never been to Church Point.

A scholar/playwright/performer, Elizabeth Brown-Guillory now serves as distinguished professor of theater at Texas Southern University. She held the post of associate provost/associate vice president for Academic and Faculty Affairs for six years and was interim dean of the Thomas F. Freeman Honors College for three. Prior to joining the faculty at Texas Southern, she held professorships at the University of South Carolina–Upstate in Spartanburg and at Dillard University in New Orleans.

When she accepted the position at the University of Houston, she became the first Black professor to join the faculty as an associate professor with tenure. She taught graduate and undergraduate courses in African/Diaspora literatures, women writers, American ethnic literatures, playwriting and American dramatic literature. While there, she won the Cooper Teaching Excellence Award and the College of Liberal Arts and Social Sciences Teaching Excellence Award and was twice awarded the English Honor Society's Sigma Tau Delta Distinguished Professor Award. After contacting 150,000 alumni, the UH Alumni Organization selected her as one of its "Phenomenal Professors."

Brown-Guillory's road to those positions was full of years of study and teaching. Born in Lake Charles, she received her bachelor and master of arts degrees from the University of Louisiana at Lafayette (then University of Southwestern Louisiana), followed by a PhD from Florida State University. Later, she traveled widely, including visits to France, China, England, Canada, Brazil, Japan, Germany, Poland, the Czech Republic, Mexico, the Bahamas, Scotland, Wales, West Africa, Accra, Ghana, Grand Cayman Islands and Barbados. Her trips were often a combination of pleasure and research, as she visited libraries and resource centers to collect plays written by underrepresented groups of women in the various locales.

Her interest in dramatic literature surfaced early as a high school teacher, Bazile Miller, recognized Brown-Guillory's talent. After giving her a book titled *How to Write a Play*, he assigned her the task of writing and directing one for the entire student body: a heavy task for a fifteen-year old. At USL, she fell under the influence of Professor Paul Nolan, who sponsored performances of student- and faculty-authored plays at an off-campus venue known as the Red Dog Saloon. In graduate school at Florida State University, Brown-Guillory studied playwriting with Jane Burroway and then went on to have over a dozen plays produced in Washington, D.C., New York City, Los Angeles, Denver, New Orleans, Houston, Cleveland, Chicago and other cities. They include *Bayou Relics*, *Saving Grace*, *Snapshots of Broken Dolls*, *Mam Phyllis*, *La Bakair*, *When the Ancestors Call* and *The Break of Day*. Her plays have won her a series of honors and awards, including residences in Illinois, Wisconsin and New York. Her work was showcased in Houston at the Ensemble Theater's "Heart of the Theater" series. As her plays have been mostly produced on college campuses and in community theaters, they are expected to attract more scholarly interest, as they are produced in larger venues.

Brown-Guillory's interest in the theater is evident in her scholarly work as well as her creative writing. As a scholar, she has published *Their Place on the Stage: Black Women Playwrights in America*, described by Eugene Kraft in an article in *Black American Literature Forum* as "a reference work important to anyone studying Black women playwrights or Black drama." Other books include *Wines in the Wilderness: Plays by African-American Women from the Harlem Renaissance to the Present*, *Women of Color: Mother Daughter Relationships in Twentieth Century Literature* and *Middle Passages and the Healing Place of History: Migration and Identity in Black Women's Literature*. She frequently publishes essays, reviews and interviews in major journals and critical anthologies. She claims her publishing success is the result of teachers along the way recognizing her talent and encouraging her to continue her research into marginalized writers, particularly Black women playwrights.

The writer has spent some time on the stage herself. Trained as a Chautauqua scholar/artist, she performs the lives of renowned Black historical figures such as Madam C.S. Walker, Josephine Baker and the opera singer Sissieretta Jones. She also performs one-woman shows based on monologues from her plays.

On the other hand, administrative work has never roused great enthusiasm in Brown-Guillory. Although she has accepted various administrative positions, they never equal the excitement she finds in teaching, writing and research. As she says, "When I was tapped to serve, I accepted reluctantly each time, recognizing that service, too, is important in our profession, though it should have parameters and not become a lifelong goal, especially if administrative work stifles completely one's true passions for the profession. When administrative teams changed, I was always delightfully happy to return fully to the classroom, to creative writing, and to research."

Brown-Guillory has also been a leader in her professional organizations and activities. She has served as president of the South Central Modern Language Association and as a member of the executive committee of the national organization the Modern Language Association. Additionally, she regularly serves as consultant to the National Endowment for the Humanities. She is founder and faculty advisor-mentor to the Houston Suitcase Theater, a faculty, staff and student troupe committed to enhancing diversity in the arts at the University of Houston. She is also founder of Erzulie, an African dance troupe at the University of Houston. Not surprisingly, she has won the UH Council of Ethnic Organizations' Outstanding Service Award.

Her work continues today with a focus on Alice Childress, whom she considers to be her literary mentor. Having spent her career studying Childress's works, Brown-Guillory has published essays about her plays and has given numerous presentations about her work at academic conferences. Currently, she is working on a book-length manuscript about the playwright and a new play titled *Kissing It Goodbye*, which is scheduled to be produced in February 2022.

Brown-Guillory's plays grow out of her small-town roots in Church Point, Louisiana. As Violet Bryan sees them, they capture the "language, habits, and values of the religious, race-conscious, Cajun/Creole people of the community in which she grew up." Through her plays, she points out their strengths and their conventions but criticizes their limitations with humor. In this way, she sees herself as preserving the rich heritage of Louisiana. As she says:

> *I have always viewed myself as a Louisiana writer, although one of my plays,* When the Ancestors Call, *was included in the anthology* Acting Up and Getting Down: Plays by African-American Texan*s. I write about people I've known and loved my whole life, and because their experiences are universal, they appeal to people in any locale of all age groups and any ethnicity. I write about what I know intimately, and that allows me to reach people who see themselves in the stories I tell about "downhome" folk from Church Point.*

All of her plays are to some extent comic social commentary on people and their cultures. They often feature old women found in Southwest Louisiana. A recurring character is the perpetually meddling Viola, whose gossiping taunts always contain an element of truth. According to Violet Bryan, Brown-Guillory says that "Sister Viola is a blend of both my grandmother and a few great aunts in my little town. I hear their voices, which are so rich that I feel compelled to keep them alive....In a strange way, they're helping me grow—to live—though they're dead. I imagine what they say or do in a given situation and their voices jump on the stage—sometimes in the raw—unguided."

Asked if any small town would provide as many memorable characters as Church Point has, she says:

> *I think any small town or large town, for that matter, could provide as much fodder for wonderful stories. The important point I want to make is that when a writer pulls back the layers and digs deeply into the lives (real or imagined) of characters, that author must focus on extrapolating the human condition and offer specifics that resonate in the lives of the general population. There is a lot of brokenness in our modern day world, as there has been in every generation previous, and I use my writing to help heal.*

With success in so many areas of her professional life, one wonders where her strongest passions lie. Does she favor teaching, creative writing or scholarship? Brown-Guillory says that the question is like asking a mother which of her several children is her favorite. She explains:

> *I am passionate about all three components of my career. In my forty-year teaching career, I have had an opportunity to transform the lives of many students. In helping them to become their best, I am uplifted and, in turn, I am encouraged to keep reaching out to students. I have been honored with five teaching excellence awards. I had some incredible teachers and professors who served as role models for me, including* [one] *who saw talent and encouraged me to change my major from history to English in my freshman year. That was a game changer in so many ways. Some years later…my major professor in the doctoral program at Florida State University encouraged me to continue my research on Black women playwrights beyond the dissertation. She said, "If not you, then who; if not now, then when?" So, I made a career of teaching and writing about women's plays. Playwriting is important to me because it allows me to tell the stories that heal and give me as much fulfillment as helping students achieve their goals.…I love everything I do and each allows me to contribute to the healing our world seeks today.*

Neither is there any question about her love of her home state. Many of her family and friends are still there, and she confesses to be there in spirit every day of her life. As she says:

I was fortunate to grow up in a farming community where whites and blacks truly were "good neighbors" to each other. I have often said that the life I recall of Southwest Louisiana I have not seen anywhere else in real time or in the literature of major or minor American writers. The wall that blocks people of different races from each other did not seem to exist in my Louisiana. I am not suggesting that we were one big homogeneous group; I'm saying we (blacks and whites) knew who we were, and we were proud of our heritage, culture without wishing to obliterate differences....In my writing, I choose to write about Louisiana and its gumbo people because my home state shaped my view of the world, namely that it is important to see people for who they are and to accept and embrace both the similarities and differences. Now, cher, *that is my Louisiana.*

MAJOR WORKS

Plays

Bayou Relics. Colorado Contemporary Drama Service, a division of Meriwether Publishing Co., 1983.

The Break of Day. In *Black Theatre in Texas.* Edited by Sandra Mayo and Ervin Holt. Austin: University of Texas Press, 2011.

La Bakair. The SUNO Review: A Journal of the Arts and Humanities 1, no. 2 (Spring 2001): 49–88.

Mam Phyllis. In *Wines in the Wilderness: Plays by African-American Women from the Harlem Renaissance to the Present.* Edited by Elizabeth Brown-Guillory. Westport, CT: Greenwood Press, 1990, 191–227.

"Saving Grace." *The Griot* 22, no. 1 (Fall 2003): 47–66.

Snapshots of Broken Dolls. Colorado Contemporary Drama Service, a division of Meriwether Publishing Co., 1987.

When the Ancestors Call. In *Black Theatre in Texas.* Edited by Sandra Mayo and Ervin Holt. Austin: University of Texas Press, 2011.

Books

Middle Passages and the Healing Place of History:
Migration and Identity in Black Women's Literature
Their Place on the Stage: Black Women Playwrights in America
Wines in the Wilderness: Plays by African-American Women
from the Harlem Renaissance to the Present
Women of Color: Mother Daughter Relationships in Twentieth Century Literature

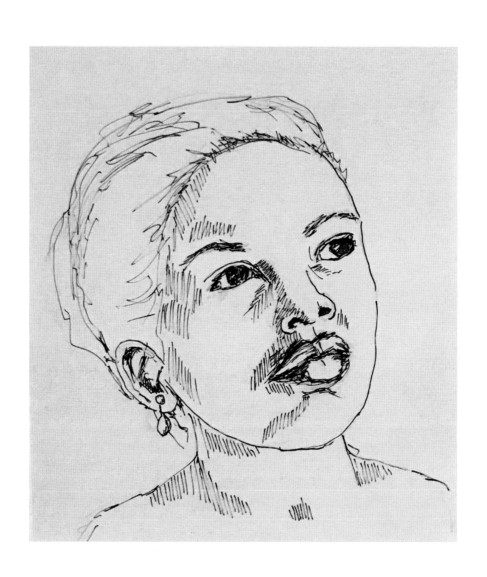

OLYMPIA VERNON

WAITING ON A CONSENSUS

Vernon's is a new African-American and Southern voice with sustaining traumatic power that magnifies the human condition.
—*Jean Thompson,* Baltimore Sun

Like Elizabeth Brown-Guillory, Olympia Vernon is the product of a small South Louisiana town, but her novels reflect a far different vision of the world than the plays of her contemporary. Her fiction is gritty, sometimes brutal, somewhat surreal and highly poetic. The images are intense and Gothic, a combination of the dreamlike and mundane. She forces the reader to face hard realities and offers little comfort in dealing with them.

Born in 1973 in Bogalusa, Louisiana, Vernon grew up in Mount Hermon, Louisiana, and Osyka, Mississippi. She wrote as a child: journals, letters, stories, whatever came to mind. As a young adult, she considered working in criminal justice, earning a BA in that field from Southeastern Louisiana University in 1999 and then going on to garner a master of fine arts degree in creative writing from Louisiana State University in 2002. She now teaches writing at Willamette University in Salem, Oregon.

Olympia Vernon has written three novels: *Eden* (2002), *Logic* (2004) and *A Killing in This Town* (2006). All have received critical notice. *Eden*, written while Vernon was in graduate school, is a coming-of-age story about a young Black girl in Mississippi who faces hard realities of race, sex and death. The novel brought Vernon early success, as it won the 2004 Richard and Hinda Rosenthal Foundation Award from the American Academy of Arts and

Letters, was nominated for a Pulitzer Prize for fiction and was selected as a Best Book of 2003 for southern reading by the *Atlanta Journal-Constitution*.

Narrated by fourteen-year-old Maddy Dangerfield, the story of the two worlds she lives in, that of her devout mother and gambling, hard-drinking father and that of her dying Aunt Pip, comes to life. It is in the latter environment that she learns the formidable strength of women and the value and cost of living one's own life. The setting is vaguely contemporary, but the events seem to take place in mythic time. The world beyond those two homes is filled with hypocrisy and scandal, but Maddy comes to realize that with knowledge and the courage to question, she can combat what is given. Ann Powers, writing in the *New York Times Book Review*, called the novel "daring [and] explosively supernatural....[*Eden* is] a startling reminder of how forceful Southern magic can be....The message is simple, though profound: love and death destroy difference, devouring us all.... Vernon's talent...is as green and growing as those country fields where her ghosts lurk."

Despite such glowing praise, other readers have found grounds for negative criticism of *Eden*. Objecting that her metaphors are vague and undefinable and that the narrative moves slowly, simply reiterating the situation without progression, some have found the novel to be unappealing. An unidentified reader writing in *Library Thing Review* commented:

> *This might be one of the worst books I've ever read. Vernon seems to be trying to write like Toni Morrison, but Vernon's story gets bogged down in an abundance of metaphors, many of which don't make sense, colloquial language, which seems authentic only in its use of clichés, and graphic language. Some of the plot elements are too similar to those in other works of literature, especially those of Morrison. For example, the men stealing Maddy's grandmother's milk is [sic] straight out of Morrison's* Beloved. *I can see what Vernon was trying to do with this novel, but I don't think it was very successful at all.*

After reading Vernon's second novel, *Logic*, Susan Larson commented that Vernon "seems drawn to the dark places where humanity faces its greatest test." The comment is justified by the novel's tale of a thirteen-year-old Black girl named Logic living in Mississippi (again) whose reality is changed by a fall from a tree. After the experience, her perceptions are clouded and strange. She feels as if there are "butterflies floating inside her." As her mother drifts away into serving as a midwife for the neighborhood, her father succumbs to paranoia and her community fails to support her, she is left to struggle in a world of her own. Ultimately, she has to deal with her burgeoning adolescence and survive in a world she is yet to understand. It is a brutal world Logic lives in, a world of poverty, ignorance and violence.

As with *Eden*, reviewers recognize in *Logic* Vernon's notable talent but are also aware that at times it seems to soar out of control. Noting the comparisons of Vernon's work to that of Toni Morrison, Rachel Howard, writing on the positive side in the *San Francisco Chronicle*, comments, "Distinctions dissolve, material associations give way to almost mystical connections, and a kind of divine oneness glows off the page. Like Logic herself, the reader is no longer earthbound but levitating in a higher reason. The effect is both bewildering and bewitching."

The reviewer for *Kirkus* comments less enthusiastically that "Vernon's vision is relentless, nearly misanthropic, often unintelligible except at a second reading." And the *USA Today* reviewer says that *Logic* "challenges the heart and the mind." Once again, an anonymous reader writing in the *Library Journal* finds fault, writing:

> *If Vernon intended to plop her readers into a world they won't understand mirroring the experiences of 13-year-old protagonist Logic Harris, a disabled girl impregnated by her father, neglected by her mother, and living in a place so remote it's as if time had stopped,* Logic *is successful, even brilliant. If, on the other hand, Vernon is going for a coherent narrative, she has failed badly.*

The verdict regarding Olympia Vernon's fiction, it would seem, is still out.

Vernon's most recent novel, *A Killing in This Town*, has met with a similarly mixed reception. Set in Bullock County, Mississippi, it is the tale of how Adam, a white boy on the eve of his thirteenth birthday, faces a bloody ritual expected of him by the Klan, that of dragging a Black man to his death. It depicts a society filled with hatred and cruelty and fear. Reluctant to wear the Klan robes made for him and carry out the social dictates of his elders, Adam is encouraged to challenge their expectations when Gill, a man haunted by his own guilt, returns to town. Ultimately, with Gill, Adam understands that he can stand up to a society poisoned by hatred and end the sanctioned cycle of violence.

Susan Larson, again writing in the *New Orleans Times-Picayune*, found *A Killing in This Town* to be praise-worthy, commenting:

Vernon's spooky magic has never been deeper or stronger....The beauty and fury of Vernon's writing burn brightly in this age-old Southern story, made new and startling by her fierce intensity, her witchy ability to cast a spell. Readers…will know they've entered a writer's original world and will find themselves haunted by its characters, its landscape and its siren song.

Publisher's Weekly, acknowledging that it "makes for lots of atmosphere," described it as "a fugue of folk idiom, blues, biblical diction and surreal imagery." Along with such encomiums have come the usual objections from readers who have found the narrative hard to follow, the metaphorical language excessive and distracting and the subject matter repugnant. Nevertheless, in 2007, the novel won the first Ernest J. Gaines Award for Literary Excellence.

Asked about her writing process, Vernon describes an experience not much less surreal than the narratives that come out of it. In an interview with James Madison Redd, she described it as highly intense and absorbing, so intense that she sometimes makes calls to family and friends to let them know before she begins that she is "going in." She said:

I remember writing Eden *and I was in another world entirely, having no concept of time (this was before I made the calls to friends and family, so you can imagine) or place or space….It was such a space that even now I don't remember much of what was going on during that time in my life— meaning in atmosphere—when it was all over, I was exhausted….When I am writing, I see the events of my characters' lives happening as though I am directing a film. I feel and smell everything. I walk through. I run. I take in an entire scene as it is revealed to me. That's when the words come. I am writing the film as the film is being portrayed; so, I have no time to stop and think of what word goes where. The film is happening and it is happening "now," and I have to keep up with it.*

Living in the world she is creating brings Vernon powerfully close to her characters. As she walks with them, hears their voices and dreams about them, they grow real. She refers to them, in fact, as her children. As she told James Madison Redd, "My characters are my children. They come and are born through me. And I am blessed to possess the feeling of having them there."

Olympia Vernon is no stranger to prizes. Along with the Gaines Award, the Richard and Hinda Rosenthal Foundation Award from the American

Academy of Arts and Letters and the nomination for a Pulitzer Prize, in 2005 she received the Louisiana Governor's Award for Professional Artist of the Year, and in 2007–08 she was named the Hallie Ford Chair in Writing at Willamette University.

Nevertheless, a consensus of opinion about Vernon's stature as a novelist is yet to be reached. Primarily, the lack of agreement seems to lie between the professional critics, who view her as a new and powerful voice from whom readers can expect fearless indictments of social injustice, and ordinary readers, who object to both her literary style and her choice of subject matter. Occasionally, there is mention of words like "early effort," "maturation" and "honing her skills," suggesting that as a relatively young writer, Vernon has room to grow, to shape her obvious talents into fiction that both critics and those who read for pleasure can approve. At present, both sets of readers wait for consensus.

Major Works

Eden
A Killing in This Town
Logic

MALAIKA FAVORITE

ARTIST AND POET

*The focus of my work is to use art as a form of meditation
on present reality and cultural investigations.*
—Malaika Favorite

If you were to Google Malaika Favorite, you would find extensive information about her art but little about her writing. Indeed, one could almost come away not knowing that she is also a well-respected poet. A poet she is, however, one who sometimes combines the two art forms into a single creation.

Born in Geismar, Louisiana, and christened Barbara as the second of nine children of Amos and Rosemary Favorite, she grew up in an environment that was partly technical and partly rural. The technical connection was through her father, who worked at the Ormet chemical complex, one of the petrochemical plants along the River Road. The plants are noted in her poem "Geismar: A River Town," including a reference to the changes the plants brought to the towns along the levee: "Everything indispensable arrived on a barge. The town / grew to accommodate / The chemical plant employees and their children / who needed new schools and a walk-in library." The rural connection came also through her father, who raised hogs in the backyard for sale and for family food. Not surprisingly, hogs have turned out to be another frequent motif in her art.

Favorite discovered art when she attended first through third grades at the all-Black Dutchtown School, where she was encouraged to develop her talent. "The teachers didn't have any money for decorating the classrooms, so they hired me and my sister," she explained to Ruth Laney. "They'd give us three dollars to make a poster. We were in the second or third grade, but we could draw. That was my first job. We'd be up all night drawing that stuff. We wanted it to be perfect."

When she was a teenager, her father agreed to pay for a correspondence course in art, the predecessor of online instruction. At that time, lessons came each month by mail. Then in 1965, when she was in the eleventh grade, a life-shaping opportunity appeared. As she tells it, one day a man came to Prairieville High School, the segregated school she was attending, to tell the students about the Freedom of Choice act, which gave individual Black students the opportunity, with their parents' permission, to attend white schools. "Instead of integrating, they came to the Black school and said, 'Who wants to go to the white school?'" She claims that despite being shy, she was ready for a change, as she was bored at the Black school. "All my friends had boyfriends, but I was a late bloomer. I wasn't into sports. I was bored to death." Several students wanted to go, but hers were the only parents who gave their permission. And so she became the first African American to integrate Ascension Parish Schools when she entered Dutchtown High School. It was not a simple step to take.

"Nothing about the experience was easy," she said. The school bus system wasn't integrated, so she was picked up by the "Black bus," which dropped her off at the white school in the morning and picked her up in the afternoon. As she explained to Laney, "There was constant harassment. A few girls treated me decent." From time to time, objects were thrown at her, a dead bird or eggs. "I'd sit down at a table in the cafeteria and everybody would get up and leave." In short, "It was a scary thing, but I wasn't gonna leave the school. I wasn't the smartest student, but I thought I had as much right to go there as anybody else."

She was not the only one affected by her change of schools. Her brother was beaten up because of it. Aware of potential for trouble, her father and brother would take turns sitting up through the night with a shotgun. The experience made its way into a poem, "Cross Burning," the third stanza of which describes that event:

> *It is difficult to sleep one eye at a time.*
> *He stations my brother at the front window*
> *with a gun while he closed both eyes for one hour.*
> *I close my other eye and dream about*
> *Jamie Pauley writing love notes to me.*
> *Then I hear my brother screaming for Daddy,*
> *hear Daddy running down the hallway,*
> *Mommy crying: "Lord, have mercy!"*
> *We all run behind her, afraid to be left alone*
> *with the fears pouring like sweat from our pores.*
>
> *Outside the darkness ignites bright red.*
> *A tall cross lights up the yard*

like a storefront Christmas tree,
beautiful in its ugliness, towering above
the young trees Daddy planted the year before,
licking up the grass, swallowing,
spitting out orange sparks.
Baby sister asks if it is fireworks,
I say yes, but it's not the Fourth of July.

Following high school, Favorite moved on to Louisiana State University, where she earned bachelor of fine arts and master of fine arts degrees. On campus, she was active in numerous organizations and causes, including giving speeches in opposition to Ku Klux Klan leader David Duke at Free Speech Alley near the Student Union. After graduating from LSU, she taught at Grambling State University, Louisiana State University and at the parish level in Napoleonville and Baton Rouge. Before returning to Geismar, Louisiana, to care for her aging mother in 2016, Favorite spent close to twenty years living in Georgia with her husband, the author and poet Anthony Kellman.

Favorite's visual art ranges from the personal to the universal. The personal side is apparent in her use of old wood-and-tin washboards that honor the work of her grandmother and aunt, who were laundresses, and of her mother, who ran the household. As she is quoted in an article in *Country Roads*, "A washboard has a historic feeling, but it also means labor. It already tells a story." Similarly, the image of a hog recalls her father's efforts to provide additional income and food for the family. By extension, they speak of family support and love. Her broader focus is defined in the artist statement found on her website, in which she says, "The focus of my work is to use art as a form of meditation on present reality and cultural investigations. As I observe the political, social, and cultural landscape of America, I offer my art as a starting point for discussion. I believe that color, form, and imagery can help us to reflect on who we are, and where we are going as a people who identify as a unified body. My series is about this identity and what it means to be a part of the American collective reality."

Favorite works in a variety of different ways: using found objects, combining folk and contemporary techniques, sometimes producing traditional works such as oils, acrylics, watercolors and lithographs. Neither are her works limited to a single material. They may be a combination of metal, wood, canvas or even household objects arranged in unique shapes. Regardless of the materials or strategies, her works take on symbolic meanings that become commentaries on social injustice, family relationships, an act of God, faith or more. In an artist's statement given to the Society 1858 Prize for Contemporary Southern Art, she says, "It is very difficult to explain a work of art, mostly because the work is its own explanation. Art is not for the immediate audience only, if it was it would be as, prop or backdrop for a play, designed to be viewed for a limited time. Visual art should be timeless. It should speak to each generation, and to each viewer as an endless dialogue that continues to inspire, fascinate and delight." The comment can be applied equally well to her poetry.

One of Favorite's more interesting innovations is the combination of her visual art and her poetry by embedding the texts in the visual images. For example, a poem may be found taking the shape of a washboard as it assumes its curves, causing the viewer to read the poem as dictated by the washboard, line by line. The poems can be described as meditations or commentaries.

Favorite's artwork can be found in numerous permanent collections, including the Morris Museum of Southern Art, Absolut Vodka, the Coca-Cola Company, Hartsfield International Airport and others. She is an artist member of the Baton Rouge Gallery and has exhibited her work with many institutions, including the Alexandria Museum of Art, Lisanby Museum (James Madison University), the Museum of Contemporary Art of Georgia, West Baton Rouge Museum, the Hilliard Art Museum in Lafayette and McKenna Museum of African-American Art. It can also be viewed on her website, www.malaikafavorite.artspan.com.

Favorite's writing has a life of its own, also. She has published three collections of poetry: *Illuminated Manuscript* (1991), *Dreaming at the Manor* (2014) and *Ascension* (2016), which was the winner of the Naomi Long Madgett Poetry Award. Her poetry, fiction and articles have appeared in numerous anthologies and journals. Despite such success, her books are not easily found these days. They are currently in short supply at major dealers. A new book, *Arrangement in Gray and Black*, a novel, is expected to be available soon from Cosmographia Books. The title alone is interesting with its reference to James McNeil Whistler's painting by the same name, more commonly known as "Whistler's Mother." According to pre-publication press releases, it is a collection of poems rooted in the Africana folkways, lore and history of Louisiana.

Ascension, her last book issued, has much the same focus. It is divided into three parts: "Ascension of Place," "Ascension of History" and "Ascension of Self." Part one has numerous poems about "the river" (the Mississippi), which serves as a distinguishing landmark as it molds the communities it touches throughout Ascension Parish. As the opening stanzas of "The River Flows Through Us," the first poem in the book, states:

> *The river flows through us*
> *Making us one.*
> *We are crabs, skirting*
> *the borders of*
> *the river's dress.*

We are bridges
stepping across
the intestine of the
Mississippi snake.
We fish ourselves out,
scale our skin
and eat our own hearts.

The opening section also has poems about family ("Momma's Daddy"), local characters ("River Preacher"), various communities in the parish ("Geismar: A River Town") and the land ("Cotton").

Part two, "Ascension of History," reaches into the past, recalling the slave trade ("Sailing Ships"), the slave experience ("Slaving for Miss Emma"), lives of slave owners ("White Ancestor House") and social injustice ("The Lynching of the Preacher"). The river returns in the third and final section of the collection, "Ascension of Self," which also offers poems of dreams, many of them lost, some survived, as in "Dream Garment." It closes with a poem titled "Victory," recalling the dark ocean passage of arriving slaves, with a refrain of "They won by dying" and "They won by living." The use of a refrain is a practice often used by Favorite. Sometimes she specifically designates that a work is "a poem in two voices," creating a musical effect much like the call-and-response pattern brought from Africa by slaves and now found in work songs and other musical forms.

Favorite's success has earned her a number of prestigious awards. Notably, she has been honored by a Puffin Foundation Grant (2008), Porter Fleming Foundation Grant (2007), Georgia Council for the Arts (1992), Special Grant for Excellence in the Arts, Delta Sigma Theta sorority (1987), Fulbright-Hays study tour, Art of India (1978) and the African-American Institute (1975).

To share the work of Malaika Favorite is to enter her world of thoughtful consideration of the present reality and culture. Whether viewing her art, reading her poetry or being engaged in a combination of the two, it means viewing the world through the critical lens of the artist/poet's vision. Her work cannot be passed off as simply beautiful or comforting. It strikes deeper and more meaningfully, looking for core meanings of what has been and what is, always with the suggestion of what should be.

MAJOR WORKS

Ascension   *Dreaming at the Manor*   *Illuminated Manuscript*

FATIMA SHAIK

A WRITER OF MANY GENRES

Fatima Shaik is in "the ranks of black women writers preserving the voice of the Afro-American experience."
—Jackson Sun, *February 21, 1988*

Reviewers are full of glowing terms to describe Fatima Shaik's writing, but a significant descriptor that is rarely used is "varied." It is, however, a highly appropriate term because, unlike some other writers who work within a single genre, Shaik writes fiction, nonfiction, narrative histories, journalism, children's books and, most recently, carefully researched history.

Shaik is a native of New Orleans who grew up in the Creole Seventh Ward with parents who were teachers in the New Orleans public schools. Her mother, from St. Martinville, was a native Louisiana French speaker and a poet. Her father, who earned a PhD from the University of Ottawa, was one of the first Black aviators in the state. Her lineage is even more interesting, as her grandfather emigrated from Bengal to the United States in the 1890s, settled in Tremé and married a Black woman of Creole and Native American descent. With such an interesting cultural background, Shaik grew up immersed in the oral histories of her Creole family and neighbors. As she explains in the introduction to *Economy Hall*:

> *I grew up learning history on porch steps, in corner groceries, during bap-tism breakfasts, and especially at the dinner table. At some point in every*

gathering, family members and friends would bring up their disappeared and deceased relatives, then launch into their history. Each spoke of the past with the passion of a man wrongfully accused of a crime who repeats over and over his account of the moment that proves his innocence.

Education was important in her family, and she attended Xavier University of Louisiana for two years before transferring to Boston University, where she completed a bachelor of science degree followed by an MA from New York University. She began her career writing for the *Miami News* and the *New Orleans Times-Picayune* and then became an assistant editor at McGraw Hill World News and editor for its "Foreign Digests." In 1991, she began teaching at St. Peter's University, a private Jesuit university in Jersey City, New Jersey, where she founded the communications degree program. She held a literature residency in the New Orleans public schools Africana Studies Program in 2002 and was a scholar in residence at New York University in 2004.

Shaik's early work foreshadowed her career to come. While working at the *Times-Picayune* between her junior and senior years in college, she delved into the paper's "morgue" and produced a piece about Marie Laveau in which she quoted from an article published in 1875. Then, as a student at Boston University, she wrote her undergraduate thesis for the School of Public Communication on the Black newspapers in nineteenth-century New Orleans. Those and similar interests would appear throughout her writing career.

Her support for literacy extends beyond her own published works. She is a member of the Writers Room in New York City and an ex-officio trustee of PEN America as co-chair of the Children's and Young Adult Books committee. After Hurricane Katrina, she headed up the effort to move a children's library from New York to the Lower Ninth Ward of New Orleans, which eventually grew into a visiting authors program for the Martin Luther King Jr. School for Science and Technology.

Shaik is a popular presenter at state book festivals and has appeared at the Tennessee Williams/New Orleans Library Festival, Louisiana Historical Association conferences, the National Conference of Social Studies, the Satchmo Fest and more. She has received awards from the National Endowment for the Humanities, the Louisiana Endowment for the Humanities, the John Anson Kittredge Fund and the Platforms Fund sponsored by the Andy Warhol and Joan Mitchell Foundations. She is the subject of an upcoming documentary, *The Bengali*, by director Kavery Kaul. In 2021, she was named Louisiana Writer of the Year by the Louisiana Center for the Book in the State Library of Louisiana, the third Black writer to be so honored. In response to the news that she was to receive the award, she said, "I am honored to be recognized by my state. Louisiana is dear to my heart and its cultural history is central to my work. Anyone who knows me knows that Louisiana is 'home.'"

Her first book, *The Mayor of New Orleans: Just Talking Jazz*, is really three novellas. All three exemplify characteristics that are more fully developed in her later fiction. The first, which gives its title to the book, tells the story of a jazz musician who unexpectedly finds himself to be an elected official. On the day of the story, he latches on to a first-time visitor to New Orleans from New York, a traveler the one-time mayor decides needs to be introduced to the city's characters and conventions. In a long, rambling story that lasts all day and most of the night, he explains how he happened to become mayor and along the way expounds on the city and his life in it. The visitor finds the experience fairly bewildering but goes along with the travelogue and the biography. The story is enjoyable because of the humor that is produced by the conflicting cultures but is also significant because of Shaik's talent for reproducing linguistic patterns of the city. It is a practice that pervades her later fiction as well.

The second novella, *Climbing Monkey Hill*, follows the observations and experiences of Levia, an adolescent girl, as she sees and hears the reactions of adults to integration of the races. It is a far cry from *The Mayor of New Orleans* in subject matter and in tone. Levia is a thoughtful young Black girl approaching maturity who is questioning racial attitudes as she hears the subject discussed in her community. The story is interesting for several reasons, one of which is that the subject that Levia ponders is usually told as a white experience. Not in *Climbing Monkey Hill*. This telling explores it from the other side, from the Black point of view, which is not a unified point of view but equally complex as that of the white. The novella ends on a hopeful note, with Levia dreaming that someday children of all colors might run to the top of Monkey Hill, the playground in the park once available only to those of pale skins.

Before Echo, the third novella, moves out of New Orleans, at least for most of the story, and into the swamps where a young girl who has been raised by her grandfather knows only a solitary and rustic life there. After his death, she goes in search of her birth mother, who she had been told was dead, only to discover an affinity for the natural world that clashes with the noisy and sinister world she discovers in the city. The opening of the narrative showcases Shaik's poetic lyricism. As she writes about Joan's life in the swamp:

A picture of bayou country is deceiving. Slow streams converge under mud to make the appearance of land that is actually water. One net of moss hangs from one hundred trees. Lightning strikes the same stump many times.

People pass the swamp's fringes in trains, on tracks that cling to the last solid ground. Out of their windows are landscapes that take the earth's colors to every periphery. Bright orange sunsets surround people like sky on an airplane. On grey foggy mornings, they ride through a dream that has no beginning or end. But time has it limits, these people know. They are expected places—Memphis by midnight, New Orleans by dawn.

Deep in the swamp animals keep the only appointments. Birds gather at high places in trees. Raccoons make their last noisy passes for food across someone's back porch before he awakes. Fish all around splash up although they cannot see the morning coming to clean the picture of day like clothes bleaching in a galvanized tub from dark grey to light grey.

For several years after Hurricane Katrina hit New Orleans, Fatima Shaik published no fiction. Then in 2015, she brought out *What Went Missing and What Got Found*, a collection of sympathetic stories about people living in a Creole neighborhood of New Orleans, some of whom make the reader smile and some who touch the heart. One is told by a mute woman who strives to live a righteous but somewhat misunderstood life. Another tells the story of a woman moved to New Orleans by her husband. She understands the culture she has moved into as little as her noisy, messy neighbors understand her, all of the misconceptions symbolized by a bountiful fig tree in her neighbor's yard that goes unharvested, its fruits lying spoiled on the ground. In another, a fireman spends a night in the Ninth Ward musing about the value of life, his and that of a body he has found after a hurricane has swept through. These people are not power brokers or great decision makers. They are ordinary people whose lives are no less complicated for being relatively powerless. Their stories, told with tenderness and empathy, ring true because of Shaik's ability to capture the idioms and rhythms of the city.

Her young adult novel, *Melitte*, delves into the eighteenth century to depict the life of a young slave girl owned by a compassionate but poor master and his sharp-tongued wife. Given their baby to care for, Melitte establishes a close bond with the child, who she ultimately discovers is her half sister. Set in the era when Louisiana was changing from French to Spanish rule, the story is filled with hardship and hope, meanness and love. The grueling physical work and damaging emotional wounds that fill Melitte's days and even her nights paint a picture of bondage and ownership that was part of the economic and social systems of the day. Carefully researched, which is characteristic of all Shaik's writing, *Melitte* is informative about Louisiana's early history, including the slave trade, plantation life and race relations.

On Mardi Gras Day is for even younger readers. It tells the story of two children's experiences on "Fat Tuesday," the day of celebration before the beginning of Lent. Brightly illustrated by Floyd Cooper, it shows in words and colorful drawings the traditions of masking, wearing costumes and viewing the floats in the parades. Particular attention is paid to the lavishly costumed Indians with their songs and tambourines, the Zulu parade and Rex while the children shout, "Throw me something, Mister!" Lunch of gumbo, fried chicken and more follows, which leads to a good nap. After some dancing of their own, the children end the day with a final joyous parade.

Shaik's other children's book, *The Jazz of Our Streets*, celebrates New Orleans's music and Tremé. Illustrated by E.B. Lewis, it follows a pattern similar to that of *On Mardi Gras Day*. Two children, a brother and sister, follow a parade and its booming drum through neighborhood streets and soon find themselves dancing in the second line. The narrative is infused with joy, aided by the rhythms and rhymes of the text, which is organized in stanzas, like the songs it celebrates. Listen to the music in these lines:

> *Then the music sways like grandmothers walk—*
> *silence, then heavy breath.*
> *The sound is like slippers slapping and scraping*
> *on the long gravel streets.*

The book ends as happily as it has spun its tale:

> *The last, loose notes of the band,*
> *are as ancient and familiar*
> *as the nearby babbling river,*
> *and they sound sweet as our own names.*
>
> *Then we go back to our porches,*
> *The morning is over,*
> *but Brother and I are feeling just fine.*
> *Because the band called us today,*
> *and we pranced, played, and swayed*
> *in the time-honored way*
> *in New Orleans, where music found feet.*
> *We marched in Tremé*
> *to the jazz of our street.*

Fatima Shaik's most recent publication, *Economy Hall*, is by far her most ambitious work. As it is a book that almost wasn't, the story behind its publication is almost as fascinating as the story it tells.

When the New Orleans building that had served as home of the Société d'Economie et d'Assistance Mutuelle (the Economy and Mutual Aid Association) was being emptied after the organization's disbanding, the armoires and chairs sold quickly, but the books and ledgers remained behind. When Shaik's father heard that they were to be thrown away, he rushed to the home of the trash hauler, where he found them, rain soaked, in the bed of a pickup truck. After rescuing them, he spread them out to dry on his front porch. Later, he deposited them in a cabinet he built for them, and there they stayed for years and years. In 1997, during a visit to New Orleans, Shaik began to examine the volumes, discovering entries written in elegant French script that dated back to 1836. She had found a part of American history that few people knew. It is that history that she reveals in *Economy Hall*.

The twenty-four volumes, composed of about three thousand handwritten pages, contained the minutes of the Société from 1836 to 1935. The project of reading, translating and understanding them soon captivated Shaik, leading her to examine other books and journals, real estate purchases and architectural surveys from those years, even finding elderly people who had danced at la Salle d'Economie. In the process, she learned that the Société was initially composed of professional free men of color who lived in the French Quarter, the Faubourg Marigny and the Tremé neighborhoods of the early nineteenth century. Later, membership was expanded to include men from throughout the city, and eventually even those with Anglo surnames and immigrants from other countries were accepted. As Shaik points out, "They were the elite of the most prosperous free Black community in the South."

The members met frequently with a mission "to help one another and teach one another while holding out a protective hand to suffering humanity." In time, they reached out to political and military leaders in Haiti, Cuba, Mexico and the United States. These books and ledgers, primary sources, not only recorded the minutes of the Société's meetings but even documented those members who had served in the Battle of New Orleans and the Civil War, Reconstruction and civil rights movement. They were, Shaik discovered, a primary record of the history of the multiracial makeup of New Orleans and a treasured Creole identity.

The Société held banquets and hosted political dignitaries, abolitionists and even mystics at meetings, debates, recitals, seances, parties and theatrical events. As the doors were open to other organizations needing a place to meet, in time it became known as a performance venue for early jazz musicians, the events for which it is best known today. The Société hosted local musicians and teachers of jazz and rented out the hall for dances that in time became legendary. As Shaik points out, over one hundred oral histories in the Hogan Jazz Archive of Tulane University mention meetings, balls and parties held at the hall. On one occasion, it gave Louis Armstrong his start in the world of music.

Shaik has meticulously researched her subject, but it reads less like a history text than a gripping narrative. Told through Ludger Boguille and his descendants, it introduces the reader to fascinating individuals who struggled with issues of slavery, war, education and more. Boguille is described as "warm, smart, open-hearted, and influential." A teacher himself, he valued the written word, as is evident in his compulsive note taking, a trait that served him well when he was secretary of the organization. With the focus on Boguille and his colleagues, *Economy Hall* becomes a human story as well as the revelation of a slice of history that had been lost.

Fatima Shaik celebrates Louisiana in her fiction, narrative history and children's books—indeed, in all she writes. That is not to say that she promotes spurious traits or exaggerates the region's attractions, for she is honest well beyond factual accuracy. Her stories, regardless of their genre, ring true and honest. They have the sound of one who knows where she is from.

MAJOR WORKS

Economy Hall: The Hidden History of a Free Black Brotherhood
The Jazz of Our Street
The Mayor of New Orleans: Just Talking Jazz
Melitte
On Mardi Gras Day
What Went Missing and What Got Found

JESMYN WARD

TELLING STORIES
ABOUT THE PEOPLE SHE LOVES

*Ward is an attentive and precise writer who dazzles with natural and
supernatural observations and lyrical details.…She continues telling stories we
need to hear with rare clarity and power.*
—O, the Oprah Magazine

Jesmyn Ward grew up in Mississippi. She still maintains a home in
Mississippi. Her fiction is set in Mississippi. Currently, however, she is
a professor of creative writing at Tulane University in New Orleans and is
working on a novel set in nineteenth-century Louisiana. That fact, coupled
with another (the fact that her hometown is only sixty miles from New
Orleans), qualifies her to join the ranks not only of her fellow Mississippi
writers but those in this state as well.

Ward was born in 1977 far from the South in Berkeley, California, but
when she was three, her family decided to move back to their home state
of Mississippi. Living in DeLisle, a small town near the Gulf Coast, she
developed the love-hate relationship with the state that still characterizes her
writing. The attitude began to develop when she was bullied at public school
by Black classmates. Help arrived when she was twelve when a wealthy
lawyer for whom her mother worked as a housekeeper offered to move her
from her segregated middle school to a private Episcopal school. As she was
the only Black student there until her senior year, she faced more bullying
that increased her desire to leave Mississippi and go to college.

College, however, was not a likely experience for Ward given her own
and her family's circumstances. Her difficulties began at birth when she

was born prematurely at just twenty-six weeks. The problems that followed were many and serious. Her mother worked as a maid, relying sometimes on food stamps to feed the family. Her father, who left the family when she was young, worked irregularly at various low-paying jobs and raised pit bulls to fight, one of which badly attacked her when she was a child.

In the 1980s, the family's situation became so dire that they were forced to move into her grandmother's house, making a total of thirteen people living in its four bedrooms. Surprisingly, Ward found it to be a happy time when "everyone told stories." It was an experience that led her to a love of reading, a practice that gave her a way to escape her circumstances. She still remembers the plucky girls who held her attention in books such as *The Secret Garden, Island of the Blue Dolphins* and *Pippi Longstocking*. She may have identified with their adventuresome spirits, but there was one big difference between Jesmyn Ward and the fictional characters she admired: they were all white, and she was Black. The message was clear. Black girls either didn't matter or were not capable of heroic action. Later, in an interview for *The Guardian*, she was to say, "You have a small array of bad choices and you pick your poison and that's your life." Unlike many of those she grew up with, and many of the characters in her books, she chose a love of books and learning. She became the first in her immediate family to go to college.

Ward went to Stanford, where she earned her bachelor's degree in English and her master's in media studies and communication, followed by an MFA in creative writing from the University of Michigan. She distinguished herself at the latter by winning five Hopwood Awards for her fiction, essays and drama. As she recalled in an NPR interview, "It made more sense for me to go to law school or go to nursing school and train myself for a profession where success was sort of guaranteed once you're done with the schooling," but when her younger brother was killed by a drunk driver in 2000, just after Ward had completed her master's degree, everything changed. "I didn't have a choice anymore," she says. "I couldn't run from that desire to tell stories, that desire to tell stories about us, and about the people I loved. I couldn't run from it anymore."

Ward's career, at least its academic side, moved steadily forward from that point on. She currently teaches at Tulane University, where she is the recipient of Tulane's Paul and Debra Gibbons Professorship. She also works closely with the New Orleans Center for the Gulf South and the Newcomb College Institute. Previously, she was an assistant professor of creative writing at the University of South Alabama. She held a Stegner Fellowship from Stanford University from 2010 to 2011 and served as the John and Renee Grisham Writer in Residence at the University of Mississippi for 2014. She is also a contributing editor for *Vanity Fair* and is a member of Black Artists for Freedom, a collective of Black workers in the culture industry dedicated to reclaiming the freedom of Black people.

After living in different parts of the country, Ward decided to return to DeLisle and raise her own children there. As she explains in her memoir, *Men We Reaped*, "I'd been homesick for so long, I really wanted to see what it was like to live as an adult in the south." She confesses that she felt bound "by a love so thick it choked me." Like most of the inhabitants, her family has lived there for generations, making her related to most everyone in town. Indeed, in *Men We Reaped* there seems to be no end to cousins.

The move back to her roots did not mean she had changed her sense of the place, her contradictory feelings of belonging and of hating that she is a part of it. As she explained in an interview with NPR's Melissa Block, "There's a feeling of ease and of knowing who I am that I feel here that I don't feel anywhere else. There's this entire web of people that I'm connected with, and I think that gives me a sense of myself that is hard for me to access when I'm not here. A way of understanding myself: who I am and where I come from, and *who* I come from." At the same time, she admits that there is much she dislikes about the place: its history of slavery and Jim Crow and sharecropping. As she told Lisa Allardice, "It's everything that I love and everything that I hate."

Ward's writing career started slowly. She recalls that when she began sending out her work for publication, she struggled to find acceptance because it was thought that people would not want to read about the kind of people she wrote about. While searching for a publisher for her first novel, *Where the Line Bleeds*—written to remember her younger brother, who was killed by a drunk driver—she began working at the University of New Orleans, where she could not escape seeing the post-Katrina destruction and the struggle of those left in the damaged neighborhoods to return to a life they once knew. Inevitably, the experience reinforced her desire to tell the stories of marginalized people. Despite her resolve, however, the seeming lack of interest in her work led her to consider giving up writing and entering a nursing program. Before she took such a step, the novel was accepted by Agate Publishing and chosen to be a Book Club Selection by *Essence* magazine. It, like the works to follow, carried out the mission she enunciated in her acceptance speech at the 2011 National Book Awards:

> *I understood that I wanted to write about the experiences of the poor, and the Black and the rural people of the South, so that the culture that margin-alized us for so long would see that our stories were as universal, our lives as fraught and lovely and important, as theirs.*

Where the Line Bleeds introduces much that is to be found in the novels that followed. For one, the setting remains the same: they all unfold in the small town of Bois Sauvage, "the fictional twin" of DeLisle. Her debut novel also set the pattern her later characters were to follow. They are southern, Black and poor. In an interview with Louis Eliot, Ward declared that she has always wanted to write about "black characters who are multidimensional, who are complicated, who are sympathetic, who have soul." The subject, too, remains the same: what it means to be poor and Black in America's rural South. Modern Mississippi, she says, "means addiction, ground-in generational poverty, living very closely with the legacy of slavery, of Jim Crow, of lynching and of intractable racism." And that is the subject she addresses from one novel to the next.

In contrast, or perhaps in balance to the stark circumstances of her characters' worlds and Ward's unflinchingly realistic depiction of them, is the lyrical quality of her prose. Laced throughout with metaphorical language, it veritably sings. Take, for example, such a statement as this one in *Salvage the Bones:* "And I can see Daddy through the window of the shed, his face shining like the flash of a fish under water when the sun hit." Or, a few pages later, she pictures a boy's embrace of a dog named China as "he curled around China like a fingernail around flesh." In fact, in an interview with Lisa Allardice, she calls herself a "failed poet," secretly writing poems that "I share with no one," but she hopes one day to publish a collection of them. Ward blames her poetic style for some of the response her work initially encountered: in the United States at the moment, she says, "people prefer cleaner, more spare, less flowery language." There is also the possibility that some readers felt that her characters would not use such poetic language.

Where the Line Bleeds begins on the celebratory day of high school graduation for twin brothers Joshua and Christopher. That day, as it turns out, is the high point of their lives, and the story that follows traces their difficulties in entering a world that does not welcome them. One finds work as a dockhand, but the other, unable to find employment, turns to selling drugs. The novel documents their descent into lives they never wanted or sought. Lisa Allardice reported in an article published in *The Guardian* that Ward admitted that in that first novel, she probably "protected" her characters from the brutal realities of their lives because she knew and cared about them too much: "So I kept pulling my punches. And later I realized that was a mistake. Life doesn't spare the kind of people who I write about, so I felt like it would be dishonest to spare my characters in that way." On publication of *Where the Line Bleeds*, *Publishers Weekly* called Ward "a fresh new voice in American literature who unflinchingly describes a world full of despair but not devoid of hope." It received a Black Caucus of the American Library Association (BCALA) Honor Award in 2009 and was shortlisted for the Virginia Commonwealth University Cabell First Novelist Award and the Hurston-Wright Legacy Award.

When Hurricane Katrina hit the Gulf Coast in 2005, Ward was forced to evacuate her flooded home. That experience and the suffering that followed were to find their way into her fiction, most notably into her second novel, *Salvage the Bones*, winner of the 2011 National Book Award, a prize she confesses to have been surprised to win since the novel had received scant attention from reviewers. In it, she once again depicts the lives of a poor Black family living on the Gulf Coast, this time covering the ten days leading up to Hurricane Katrina, the day of the storm and the day after. There is Esch, a pregnant teenager, and her three brothers, one a hopeful basketball player who loses his chance to play before athletic scouts, another obsessed with raising a fighting pit bull and the third a young hanger-on. The father is an inattentive, often drunk widower who scrambles to keep food on the table. When the hurricane hits, they lose what little they have—all they have except their intense bonds and their fierce love for one another.

A particularly interesting element of the narrative is that Esch is doing her summer reading assignment, Edith Hamilton's *Mythology*. After reading the chapter titled "Eight Brief Tales of Lovers" and finding the story of Jason and the Argonauts, she sees her infatuation with Manny as similar to Medea's passion for Jason. Explaining Esch's fascination with the Greek mythological figure, Ward told Elizabeth Hoover of *The Paris Review* the following:

> *It* infuriates *me that the work of white American writers can be universal and lay claim to classic texts, while Black and female authors are ghetto-ized as "other." I wanted to align Esch with that classic text, with the universal figure of Medea, the antihero, to claim that tradition as part of my Western literary heritage. The stories I write are particular to my community and my people, which means the details are particular to our circumstances, but the larger story of the survivor, the savage, is essentially a universal, human one.*

As in her previous work, Ward tells the story of Esch and her family in vibrant prose. Metaphors abound. They enrich the approach of the hurricane: "There is only the sound of the wind like a snake big enough to swallow the world sliding against mountains." They explain Skeetah's anticipated joy at the return of his beloved dog, China: "And when he sees her, his face will break and run water, and it will wear away, like water does, the heart of stone left by her leaving." Even the fighting dogs become metaphoric: "She is fire. China flings her head back into the air as if eating oxygen, gaining strength, and burns back down to Kilo and takes his neck in her teeth. She bears down, curling to him, a loving flame, and licks....Fire evaporates water."

Following the successful launch of her first two novels, Ward turned to nonfiction, publishing in 2013 *Men We Reaped*, a memoir that she says was written as a love letter to her family. It is built around the violent early deaths of five young men of her community, including that of her brother. Grief, she told Lisa Allardice nearly two decades later, "never goes away. I tell friends of mine who experience the death of someone close to them: 'You will never stop waiting for that person to walk through the door, but you learn how to live with it.'" She dealt with it by writing about it. Calling it the hardest thing she has ever written, she tells not only the story of five young men lost too early, but, as she states in the prologue:

> [It is] *the story of my town, and the history of my community....My hope is that learning something about our lives and the lives of the people in my community will mean that when I get to the heart, when my marches through the past and backwards from the present meet in the middle with my brother's death, I'll understand a bit better why this epidemic happened, about how the history of racism and economic inequity and lapsed public and personal responsibility festered and turned sour and spread here.*

Sing, Unburied, Sing, Ward's third novel, also tells a story of limited possibilities, bad choices and loss. The narrative this time is built around three generations of a family composed of a dying grandmother, a grandfather who struggles to mentor his grandson, a wayward daughter and her children, Michaela and Jojo, a young boy struggling to discover who he is and what he can become. Then, too, there are the dead spirits who visit from time to time, reminding all that the past lives with us and in us. Introducing that idea at the opening of the novel is the epigraph from Eudora Welty: "The memory is a living thing—it too is in transit. But during its moment, all that is remembered joins, and lives—the old and the young, the past and the present, the living and the dead."

There is love in the family, but there is also strife and pain and grief and misunderstanding. Leonie, the daughter (and mother of Jojo and Kayla), is a terrible parent who unfailingly makes the wrong choices. Scarred by having grown up Black, she is obsessed with Michael, the father of her children, leaving Jojo to care for his younger sister, which he does with tenderness and love. Pop, the grandfather, cares for his wife, strives to show his grandson what it is to be a man and tries to hold the family together as best he can.

Hanging like a shadow over the family is Parchman Prison, the oldest prison in Mississippi and reputed to be the toughest in the country. Inmates' punishment for infraction of rules at that time was severe, "Black Annie" being the name given to the black leather strap used to discipline them. In an NPR episode of *Author Interviews*, Ward says, "So much about that place reveals the essence of the worst of Mississippi. Parchman prisoners were treated like slaves: They were worked and worked and worked and worked, and they were starved, and they were beaten. They were tortured."

In *Sing, Unburied, Sing*, Pop has spent time in Parchman, time that is recalled in his stories of Richie, a young boy he befriended there, and the ghost of Richie himself, who in appearances to Jojo speaks about the horrors he has witnessed and experienced in the prison. In the NPR interview, Ward explained, "I thought, 'This person has to speak. This person has to have agency, the kind of agency that [inmates] didn't have when they were alive.'" Writing Richie's story, Ward says, "almost feels like I'm righting a wrong, in a fictional way. I mean, this is like putting a Band-Aid over an amputation. I understand that this is a small remedy. But I think it is a remedy." Parchman makes a contemporary appearance too, as Michael is being released from it. Throughout the narrative, it is a reminder of historic social inequality and lost opportunities.

Refuting concerns that the reading public would not identify with characters like those Ward creates are the prizes and honors the novel has received. In addition to being heaped with praise from noted writers and reviewers, Ward was awarded a second National Book Award for it, which made her the first woman to win two National Book Awards for Fiction. The novel also won an Anisfield-Wolf Book Award and was named one of the Ten Best Books of 2017 by the *New York Times* and *Time*. The *Washington Post* and *Publishers Weekly* also called *Sing* one of the year's best books.

Ward turned to editing in 2016 with *The Fire This Time: A New Generation Speaks about Race*, which NPR named one of the best books of the year. Triggered by the death of the Black teenager Trayvon Martin in 2012, and building on James Baldwin's 1963 examination of race in America, it is an anthology featuring essays and poems about race from such imminent Black writers and thinkers as Edwidge Danticat, Natasha Trethewey, Isabel Wilkerson, Mitchell S. Jackson, Kiese Laymon, Claudia Rankine and Jesmyn Ward.

One of Ward's latest books is *Navigate Your Stars*, an adaptation of her 2018 Tulane University commencement speech that in its published form is lavishly illustrated by Gina Triplett. In it, Ward champions the value of hard work, persistence, lifelong learning and respect for oneself and others. As she says in the conclusion:

Hold fast to your oars, hoist the sail to the wind, read the pictures in the stars, look beyond the horizon to that which you can't see but dimly sense in your future: the curving inlet, the sandy beach. Know that even those calm waters may harbor boulders, craggy rocks intent on rending the bottom of your boat, that when you land you may find your legs too weak to walk well, still shaky from the sea, and that the soil may have its own perils. But know that this is life.

Currently, Ward is working on a novel set in the past but not set in Beau Sauvage, both choices a first for her. It takes place in New Orleans in the early 1800s as the slave trade is flourishing. She explains her decision in Lisa Allardice's interview published in *The Guardian* by saying that those in power in the United States are "invested in sanitizing and erasing the past," denying its impact on the present.

They keep insisting that racism does not exist, that there's a level playing field. That we are all born with the same opportunities. If people are writing about slavery, I think it is because we want to push back against that narrative. The narrative serves them. It makes it seem like we chose our poverty, or we deserve our poverty; we deserve our ill-equipped, dangerous playgrounds, and we deserve our horrible educations and we deserve to be hungry.

Her writing priorities, it would seem, have not changed, even if the setting has. Another element that hasn't changed is the critical reception of her work. The honors and awards that Jesmyn Ward has received are many and prestigious. Among the most esteemed are the MacArthur Foundation Genius Grant and two National Book Awards. The Genius award was given for her work "exploring the enduring bonds of community and familial love among poor Americans of the rural South against a landscape of circumscribed possibilities and lost potential." *Salvage the Bones* was also given the Alex Award, which honors ten books each year that resonate with young adults ages twelve through eighteen. Commenting on the winning books that year in *School Library Journal*, former Alex Award committee chair Angela Carstensen described *Salvage the Bones* as a novel with "a small but intense following—each reader has passed the book to a friend." *Sing, Unburied, Sing* won an Anisfield-Wolf Book Award. In 2012, *Men We Reaped*, which was a finalist for the National Book Critics Circle Award, won the Chicago Tribune Heartland Prize and the Media for a Just Society Award. In 2016, Ward won the Strauss Living Award, given every five years by the American Academy of Arts and Letters for literary excellence, and in 2018, she was recognized as one of *Time*'s 100 Most Influential People.

Meanwhile, she remains in DeLisle, a decision that she continues to question as she raises her two young children, Noemie and Brando, alone following the death of her husband due to the coronavirus in January 2020, the experience she recalls in "On Witness and Respair: Personal Tragedy Followed by Pandemic." It is a document that honors her "beloved" but then broadens its focus to mourn other Black lives lost due to social injustice: Breonna, Trayvon, Tamir. She grieves for them and for those who mourn them, then finds strength in the notice given to Black lives springing to life across the country and the world. She ends with resolve to press on in her fight against social inequities and wrongdoing.

Ward now sends her five-year-old daughter to the same school she attended and feels the same closeness to the land, yet she cannot escape concerns about the future. As reported in *Gulf News*, she says she has yet to get used "to this idea of living in this place that consistently devalues me and people like me in big ways and in little ways every day."

Despite her fears for the future, she continues to hope. As she reported in that same interview:

> *But if I did not hope I would not be able to do what I do. But I don't think it is an intelligent hope, I think it is a necessary hope. And maybe that's what the people in our past did, my ancestors who were enslaved. It wasn't an intelligent hope that they had for freedom or that their children might live different lives than they did, but I think they had to hope to keep going.*

And so she keeps on going, writing for those she grew up with and for her younger self, the girl who felt silenced and "erased" by the world. Through her characters and their stories, she pushes readers to see marginalized people as human beings who undergo universal experiences, people who love and suffer and rejoice and simply "keep going."

Major Works

Commencement address, Tulane University
The Fire This Time: A New Generation Speaks about Race (editor)
Men We Reaped
Navigate Your Stars
"On Witness and Respair: A Personal Tragedy Followed by Pandemic"
Salvage the Bones
Sing, Unburied, Sing
Where the Line Bleeds

LADEE HUBBARD

INTRODUCING THE RIBKINS

For sheer reading pleasure Ladee Hubbard's original and wildly inventive novel is in a class by itself.
—*Toni Morrison*

Ladee Hubbard is another "out-of-stater" who has come to Louisiana as part of the Tulane University faculty. In 2003, Hubbard moved to New Orleans to teach in its Africana and African Diaspora Studies Department. Despite having lived in a variety of places in the world, she claims to feel most at home in New Orleans, where she has survived Katrina and raised her three children with her husband and fellow Tulane professor, Christopher Dunn. Nevertheless, she is hesitant to call herself a "southern writer," as she claims its ethos doesn't really impact her work. Recognizing that she does not fit the traditional stereotype of the southern man of letters, she was quoted in *The Guardian* as saying, "There are a lot of southern writers who are not old white guys in linen suits, but maybe they don't get so much attention. Maybe the image needs updating." She was born in Cambridge, Massachusetts, in 1970, but it is the summers spent with her grandparents in Florida and the U.S. Virgin Islands that are evident in her debut novel, *The Talented Ribkins*.

Before coming to Louisiana, Hubbard earned a BA from Princeton University, where she was mentored by the Nobel Prize–winning author Toni Morrison. Following Princeton, she completed an MFA in dramatic writing from New York University and an MFA in creative writing from the University of Wisconsin.

The Talented Ribkins, her first novel, is an auspicious beginning for Hubbard's career, as it was given the Ernest J. Gaines Award for Literary Excellence in 2017. It was inspired by W.E.B. Du Bois's 1903 essay "The Talented Tenth," first published in *The Negro Problem*, in which he argued for the higher education of African Americans. He reasoned that if they are to be able to reach their potential, they need a classical education. He does not deny that industrial training is effective in teaching technical skills but asserts that it is does not create men. To educate the best minds of the race would be to contribute to the well-being of all.

Hubbard's imagination takes Du Bois's ideas on a wild ride through Florida as Johnny Ribkins discovers he has a niece, Eloise, a ten-year-old who lives with Meredith, her mother, and never knew her father. When Meredith must leave town for a week to go on a job, Johnny agrees to watch out for Eloise during her mother's absence. That means taking her with him as he moves from place to place in an effort to meet a weeklong deadline to repay a debt he owes by digging up illegally acquired money he buried years earlier. As they travel and dig, Johnny and Eloise explore what it means to be a family, what became of the civil rights movement, what race and society mean in America and what is honorable behavior. In the course of their travels and conversations, there are moments of humor, nostalgia, regret and even joy.

As Eloise and Johnny move from place to place, they visit with family members and friends of Johnny's youth. With each reacquaintance, Johnny (who is based on Hubbard's own grandfather) is made aware of lost intentions and wasted opportunities. The family turns out to be a collection of social misfits, characterized primarily by what they see as their special talents. And while those "special gifts" cause them trouble from time to time, they give their owners a sense of being marked by a particular destiny, although what that is to be is often hard to see. The friends from the past turn out to be members of a group once known as the Justice Committee, an organization dedicated to supporting the civil rights movement and generally righting the wrongs of society. They get no credit or gratitude for their good intentions and work and, indeed, are mostly overlooked in their predominately white world, and although their later lives are not based on such high ideals, they at one time tried to make the world a better place.

Some of the tools they use are their special talents, abilities that resemble those of comic book heroes. Even "The Rib King," the family patriarch, had a superb sense of smell that gave him that title. Johnny's father could see colors no one else could see. Generations later, Eloise has the unique ability to catch anything that is thrown at her and indeed to snatch things out of other people's hands at a surprising distance. Her father was known for his special ability to climb buildings. Johnny, accepted as the smartest of the family, having what Bertrand calls "natural brilliance," can make precise maps of places he's never been. (They allow Black drivers to navigate safely through racially segregated territories.) Cousin Bertrand, nicknamed "Captain Dynamite," can "spit firecrackers," and Aunt Simone can alter her appearance at will. Another friend from the past is known as "Flash" for his running ability, and yet another is nicknamed "The Hammer" because while her left hand looks normal, her right hand is said to resemble a sledgehammer. As they all come to understand, "No one's gift was easy, but for the person who had received it, it was a source of strength and strange comfort that was difficult to understand and even harder to explain." What to do with such unusual gifts? How to use them in the real world and how they contribute to one's identity become important, and charming, aspects of Eloise's development.

At this early stage of her career, Ladee Hubbard has already collected an impressive number of honors and awards. In addition to the Ernest J. Gaines Award for Literary Excellence, she has been the recipient of a Rona Jaffe Foundation Writers' Award, the Sustainable Arts Foundation Promise Award and the Hurston-Wright Legacy Award for Debut Fiction. She has been awarded fellowships by such prestigious institutions as the MacDowell Colony, the Callaloo Creative Writers Workshop and the Napa Valley Writers Conference. In addition, she has held residencies at Sacatar Foundation Brazil, Hedgebrook Foundation and the Hambidge Center.

Judging from the response to *The Talented Ribkins*, there are more awards to come. It will be interesting to see if Hubbard gives us more characters like those in this first novel, people who do the best they can with what they have, people who are not always sure of what they should be doing but who persevere in making a difference—people with special talents.

MAJOR WORK

The Talented Ribkins

SARAH BROOM

A NEW VOICE IS HEARD

Alternating gracefully between immediacy and critical distance she leaves us with deep insight not just into her own family, her own community, but into governance, justice, and inequality in the round.
—Dwight Gamere

Sarah Broom may have produced fewer publications than most of the other writers included here, but she is no less renowned. Her debut book, a memoir titled *The Yellow House*, won the National Book Award for 2019, bringing with it widespread notice. It received pre-publication accolades in such prestigious newspapers and journals as the *New York Times*, the *Star Tribune*, *Entertainment Weekly*, *Time* and the *New York Times Magazine*. Writing in the first, Dwight Garmere spoke for dozens of critics to come, saying, "This is a major book that I suspect will come to be considered among the essential memoirs of this vexing decade." Evidence that it has already attained that status lies in the fact that it was named one of the "10 Best Books of 2019" by the *New York Times Book Review* and the *Washington Post*, along with praise from the *Seattle Times*, Chicago Public Library, the *Chicago Tribune* and *Slate*. The *Washington Post*, NPR's *Book Concierge*, NPR's *Fresh Air*, *The Guardian*, *BookPage* and the New York Public Library named it a Best Book of 2019, and LitHub called it the Best Memoir of the Decade. Novelist Heidi Julavits remarked, "I already consider her [Sarah Broom] to be one of America's most important and influential writers."

Broom, like a number of other women writers, is a native of New Orleans, which, as a matter of fact, becomes a major player in *The Yellow House*. She grew up the youngest of twelve children in New Orleans East. After graduating from Word of Faith Academy, she moved on to the University of North Texas, where she studied anthropology and mass communication, which led to a master's degree in journalism at the University of California–Berkeley.

She has always been a reader. When she was a child, her mother would buy her every book that had the name "Sarah" in the title, including Catherine McKinley's *The Book of Sarahs*. As she told Jillian Tamaki:

> *I lived for the Scholastic Book Fairs. Me and my mother made a job out of circling all the books I would buy if our budget were unlimited, then narrowed it way way down. I loved Shel Silverstein's* Where the Sidewalk Ends, *in particular. The other one I memorized and quoted from—in completely inappropriate childhood situations—was* Aesop's Fables. *I had a hardcover special edition with the best drawings. To this day, I miss that childhood copy. My mother taught us that books were a road to elsewhere—a means of deepening.*

The connection with books has lasted, and as ritual, she and her partner, Dee Rees, now read to each other most nights. In the interview with Tamaki, she stated that she especially enjoys those works in which "the writing and the story are equally captivating. I am most drawn to philosophical texts that ask existential questions. And when within this same kind of book, the writer makes me laugh? Joy!" Curiously, her taste runs to fiction but avoids the memoir. Some of her favorite authors include Saidiya Hartman, Kiese Laymon, Natasha Trethewey, Rachel Kaadzi Ghansah, Jesmyn Ward, Walton Muyumba, Maggie Nelson, Wendy S. Walters, Lynell George, Angela Flournoy and Kaitlyn Greenidge. And she reads *One Hundred Years of Solitude* at least once a year.

Broom began her writing career as a journalist working in Rhode Island, Dallas, New Orleans and Hong Kong (for *Time* Asia). Before *The Yellow House* took shape, she published articles in a number of prestigious magazines, including *The New Yorker*, *O, The Oprah Magazine* and the *New York Times Magazine*, and her reputation began to grow. In 2016, she received a Creative Nonfiction Grant from the Whiting Foundation. She was also a finalist for the New York Foundation for the Arts Fellowship in Creative Nonfiction and won fellowships at Djerassi Resident Artists Program and the MacDowell Colony.

The memoir itself was begun long before it was accepted by Grove Press. It was started as Broom's written musings and remembrances of growing up in New Orleans East: the people she knew there, her family, her neighborhood. At the center of this multigenerational story is the yellow house, Broom's childhood home, bought in 1961 by Ivory Mae, Broom's mother, in what was considered a growing area. Instead of prosperous expansion, however, the neighborhood became overrun with crime and poverty in the 1980s. When Hurricane Katrina struck in 2005, the house, full of rotting boards, a shaky staircase, electrical problems and unfinished repair projects, was washed away. Ultimately, the notes became the story of Broom's family and her community, intertwined and inseparable.

Publishers as well as family members were somewhat puzzled by Broom's intention to write not just a memoir of a family or a childhood but of a place as well. Why be concerned with the deterioration of an ignored suburb, a longtime victim of civic indifference and poor city planning, when one is writing about family? Old photographs of holidays and special occasions might be appropriate, but why be concerned with the loss of residential zoning or intentional disenfranchisement? Write about one or the other, publishers said, but not about both. On top of those disqualifiers, no history had ever been written of that area, and there seemed to be little interest in having one. Broom, however, saw the connections between her family's experience and what was happening to society at large. She saw that those collective experiences in the long run constitute history, and she persevered, in the end telling both stories, inextricably intertwined as they are. In a larger context, it became a commentary on the country at large. As Shannon Gibney wrote in the S*tar Tribune*, "[It] essentially told the story of Black America in one fell swoop."

It was Hurricane Katrina that destroyed the yellow house, but Broom warns readers not to think of the book as centered on that one event. While its impact on her family, her neighborhood, city and state were huge, she points out that it was no singular catastrophe. "When we boil Katrina down to a weather event, we really miss the point." According to Lauren Leblanc, writing in *The Atlantic*, Broom commented, "It's so crucially important for me to put Katrina in context, to situate it as one in a long line of things that are literally baked into the soil of this place."

So what was the process of putting the story of a family, an ignored suburb of a city and a massively destructive hurricane together? In an interview with Brad Listi, Broom compared it to building a house. As she explained it:

I was thinking about the book as a sort of house, that needs a specific architecture. When you go to someone's house, you don't just bust in and end up in someone's bedroom, right? There is a pathway you follow. How do you set up thresholds in a book? How does the reader feel when they're moving through it? What's the familial space and the public space? It came to me at the very beginning that I need to be contextualizing it in that way.

One of the first things I did was to get these index cards and write each room of the house, because the house I grew up in was a camelback shotgun. They call it a railroad apartment in New York. I remember writing on each of these notecards each room of the house—living room, mom's and dad's room, kitchen, small bathroom—and then laying the cards out on the floor and just looking at them for a really long time and thinking, What are the clues here for how I can organize this book?

The process may have been unusual, but it was obviously effective. Rarely does a first book garner the attention that this one has. Perhaps it appeared at a propitious time. Perhaps the author's lyrical style that carries its compelling stories of family history, sociology, natural disaster and personal growth would have captured public attention at any time. Regardless of the cause, *The Yellow House* has catapulted Sarah Broom into the roster of Louisiana's outstanding writers.

MAJOR WORK

The Yellow House

QUOTED SOURCES

ALICE RUTH MOORE DUNBAR-NELSON

Dunbar-Nelson, Alice. "Anarchy Alley." *Violets and Other Tales*. *The Monthly Review*, 1895.

———. "A Carnival Jangle." In *The Goodness of St. Roque*. 1899. Repr., CreateSpace Independent Publishing Platform, 2015.

———. *Give Us This Day: The Diary of Alice Dunbar-Nelson*. New York: W.W. Norton, 1985.

———. "On the Bayou Bridge." In *The Works of Alice Dunbar-Nelson*, vol. 3, edited by Gloria T. Hull. Oxford: Oxford University Press, 1988.

Gordon, Eugene. "Survey of the Negro Press." *Opportunity Magazine*, 1917.

Hull, Gloria. *Color, Sex, and Poetry: Three Women Writers of the Harlem Renaissance*. Bloomington: Indiana University Press, 1987.

———. Introduction to *Give Us This Day: The Diary of Alice Dunbar-Nelson*, edited by Gloria T. Hull. New York: W.W. Norton, 1985.

"Review." *Pittsburgh Christian Advocate*, December 21, 1899.

SYBIL KEIN

Kein, Sybil. *Gombo People*. Repr., Leo J. Hall, 1981.

———. "The Use of Louisiana Creole in Southern Literature." In *Creole*, edited by Sybil Kein. Baton Rouge: Louisiana State University Press, 2009.

Morton, Mary L. "Creole Culture in the Poetry of Sybil Kein." In *Creole*, edited by Sybil Kein. Baton Rouge: Louisiana State University Press, 2009.

PINKIE GORDON LANE

Harris, Kelly A. "*I Never Scream*: The Quiet Poems and Powerful Legacy of Pinkie Gordon Lane." *64 Parishes*, Summer 2018.

Hero, Danella P. *Louisiana Literature*. Quoted in "I Never Scream: The Quiet Poems and Powerful Legacy of Pinkie Gordon Lane." *64 Parishes*, Summer 2018.

Jones, Carolyn M. "Intimacy and Distance: The Poetry of Pinkie Gordon Lane." In *Louisiana Culture from the Colonial Era to Katrina (Southern Literary Studies)*, edited by John Lowe. Baton Rouge: Louisiana State University Press, 2008.

Lane, Pinkie Gordon. "I Am Looking at Music." In *Girl at the Window*. Baton Rouge: Louisiana State University Press, 1991.

———. "On Being Head of the English Department." In *I Never Scream: New and Selected Poems*. Detroit: Lotus Press, 1985.

———. "A Quiet Poem." In *I Never Scream: New and Selected Poems*. Detroit: Lotus Press, 1985.

———. "While Working towards the PhD Degree." In *Wind Thoughts*. Fort Smith, AR: South and West, Inc., 1972.

BRENDA MARIE OSBEY

Bryan, Violet Harrington. "Evocations of Place and Culture in the Works of Four Contemporary Black Louisiana Writers: Brenda Osbey, Sybil Kein, Elizabeth Brown-Guillory, and Pinkie Gordon Lane." *Louisiana Literature* (1987): 49–60.

———. *Mississippi Quarterly* 40 (1986–87): 33–45.

Hernton, Calvin C. *Parnassus*. Spring 1985.

Lowe, John. "Mapping a Starry Poetics: The Achievement of Brenda Marie Osbey." In *Summoning Our Saints*, 1–20. New York: Lexington Books, 2019.

Lowe, John, and Jefferson Humphries, eds. "An Interview with Brenda Marie Osbey." In *The Future of Southern Letters*. New York: Oxford University Press, 1996.

Rushing, Andrea Benton. "Wild and Holy Women in the Poetry of Brenda Marie Osbey." In *Summoning Our Saints*. New York: Lexington Books, 2019.

MONA LISA SALOY

Belden, Tony. Publicity from Truman State University Press. Quoted on back cover of *Second Line Home*.

Christy, Judy. *Shreveport Times*, February 24, 2016.

Reed, Ishmael. 2005 T.S. Eliot Prize judge.

Sakakeeny, Matt. "Jazz Funerals and Second Line Parades." *64 Parishes*. Louisiana Endowment for the Humanities, Summer 2019.

Saloy, Mona Lisa. Personal interview, September 15, 2020.

ELIZABETH BROWN-GUILLORY

All undocumented quotations are taken from an online interview with Elizabeth Brown-Guillory.

Bryan, Violet Harrington. "Evocations of Place and Culture in the Works of Four Black Louisiana Writers: Brenda Marie Osbey, Sybil Kein, Elizabeth Brown-Guillory, and Pinkie Gordon Lane." *Louisiana Literature Review* 4, no. 2 (1987): 49–80.

Kraft, Eugene. "Reviewed Work: *Their Place on the Stage: Black Women Playwrights in America*, by Elizabeth Brown-Guillory." *Black American Literature Forum* 24, no 1 (Spring 1990): 161–63.

OLYMPIA VERNON

Howard, Rachel. *San Francisco Chronicle*.

Kirkus Reviews. May 20, 2010.

Larson, Susan. "Review of A Killing in This Town." *New Orleans Times-Picayune*. Quoted on Grove Atlantic website.

———. "Review of *Logic*." *New Orleans Times-Picayune*. Quoted on Grove Atlantic website.

Powers, Ann. *New York Times Book Review*.

Publishers Weekly. Quoted on Grove Atlantic website.

Redd, James Madison. "Olympia Vernon: The Gift of Writing." *Prairie Schooner*, March 25, 2013.
Unidentified review of *Logic* on *USA Today* website.
Unidentified user review of *Logic* in *Library Journal*, posted in Google Books, March 1, 2004.
Unidentified writer posted in Google Books from *Library Thing Review*, n.d.

Malaika Favorite

Artist statement, Society 1858 Prize for Contemporary Southern Art.
Laney, Ruth. "An Angel in *Ascension*." *Country Roads*, March 22, 2019.
malaikafavorite.artspan.com.

Fatima Shaik

Shaik, Fatima. *Economy Hall: The Hidden History of a Free Black Brotherhood.* New Orleans: Historic New Orleans Collection, 2021.

Jesmyn Ward

Acceptance speech at National Book Awards 2011, National Book Foundation.
Allardice, Lisa. "Black Girls Are Silenced and Misunderstood." *Gulf News*, May 23, 2018.
———. "Interview with Jesmyn Ward." *The Guardian* (U.S. edition), May 11, 2018.
Block, Melissa. *Author Interviews*. NPR. August 31, 2017.
Eliot, Louis. "Ghosts of History: An Interview with Jesmyn Ward." *Bomb*, November 19, 2017.
Hoover, Elizabeth. "Jesmyn Ward on *Salvage the Bones*." *The Paris Review*, August 30, 2011.
"Review of *Where the Line Bleeds*." *Publishers Weekly*, September 22, 2008.
Ward, Jesmyn. *Men We Reaped*. New York: Bloomsbury, 2013.
Welty, Eudora. *One Writer's Beginnings*. New York: Scribner, 1983.

LADEE HUBBARD

Lea, Richard. Interview with Laree Hubbard. *The Guardian* (U.S. edition), September 14, 2017.

SARAH BROOM

Garmere, Dwight. *New York Times*, August 5, 2019.

Gibney, Shannon. "Review: 'The Yellow House' by Sarah Broom." *Star Tribune*, August 9, 2019.

Julavits, Heidi. "7 Highly Anticipated Books to Get You Through the Dog Days of August." *Los Angeles Times.* Quoted in online publicity materials.

LeBlanc, Lauren. "*The Yellow House*: A Historical Feat." *The Atlantic*, September 25, 2019.

Tamaki, Jillian. *New York Times*, July 9, 2020.

ABOUT THE AUTHOR

Ann B. Dobie is professor emerita of English at the University of Louisiana at Lafayette, where she directed graduate studies in rhetoric and the university's writing-across-the-curriculum program. She has also directed a summer institute at the University of Vermont and worked with the Malta Writing Programme in Valetta, Malta. In 2002, she chaired the One Book, One City program "Lafayette Reads Ernest Gaines."

She is the author (or co-author) of fourteen books, compiler and editor of three literary anthologies and author of numerous articles on literature and composition. For thirteen years, she served as founder and director of the National Writing Project of Acadiana. She is a contributor to the Literature Section of KnowLA, an online encyclopedia of Louisiana history and culture sponsored by the Louisiana Endowment for the Humanities.